What Readers Are Saying

LIVING ON THE PATH OF FREEDOM

Gail Porter's *Living on the Path of Freedom: Leaving Fear of Rejection Behind* brings together real, raw stories of those who've faced rejection. Each account serves up hope, redemption, rescue, and release as each storyteller relates their escape from the strangling grip of past and present rejection and finds healing and peace. Included are chapter challenges that allow readers to connect with God and plan their own path to freedom. If you feel anchored to rejection, Gail offers a way to be set free.

—Donna Mumma
Author of *Fresh Scars*

Wow. Gail Porter's book *Living on the Path of Freedom: Leaving Fear of Rejection Behind* compels us to examine our lives for the snares that trap us and keep us from living in the freedom God desires for us. Gail openly and honestly shares her story and those of others who struggle with fear of rejection. This will help readers to reach deep into our pasts to find freedom that allows us to live life to the fullest. The variety of stories will touch you on many levels. Bravo, Gail. You have written a winner.

—Patricia Hartman
Forensic CPA and author of *Poisoned* and
A Funny Thing Happened on My Journey to Heaven

Rejection comes in various shapes and sizes and at different times in our lives. Childhood trauma can follow us into adulthood and often leads to poor decisions and life choices. It takes courage to face a basketful of hurts and rejections and change the status quo of our lives. Gail Porter's book *Living on the Path of Freedom: Leaving Fear of Rejection Behind* tackles these often-debilitating rejections through individual accounts of people who faced their pain and lived to tell the story of God's redemption and restoration. When we exist under a cloud of hurt and pain, we feel as if we're the only person with scars. Gail's book gently shows us a vast community of recovering rejectees.

—Sharron K. Cosby
Speaker and award-winning author of
Praying for Your Addicted Loved One: 90 in 90

Gail Porter's *Living on the Path of Freedom: Leaving Fear of Rejection Behind* offers a ray of sunshine and hope. This book touched my heart and was difficult to put down. Gail did a beautiful job of capturing the essence of ten heartbreaking yet redemptive stories of survival. Each is guaranteed to inspire and uplift. I felt as if I'd met each person myself. Even if you've never experienced rejection, this new book will give you a big dose of hope for healing in any difficult situation you may ever face.

—Dena Yohe
Award-winning author of *You Are Not Alone*
Cofounder of Hope for Hurting Parents

Authenticity is a common buzzword. However, the path toward an authentic life is often littered with the fear of rejection. In *Living on the Path of Freedom: Leaving Fear of Rejection Behind*, Gail gently leads the reader on a personal journey through her own experiences and those of her friends. Together, they find ways to recognize their fears and release them to God. The personal stories, journal prompts, prayers, and Scripture all lead to healing, forgiveness, and a truly authentic relationship with God as you trust Him with your most intimate fears.

—Lisa Worthey Smith
Amazon best-selling and multiple award-winning author
of the Elijah Mandate series

Author Gail Porter experienced a lifelong struggle with fear of rejection. As a result, she built an impenetrable wall around her heart, shutting out authentic personal relationships. In her book *Living on the Path of Freedom: Leaving Fear of Rejection Behind*, Gail shares her personal struggle in facing a painful past. She reveals how her surrender to the healing touch of the Holy Spirit broke the strongholds of shame that caused captivity. She now walks in authentic freedom with her identity based on Christ rather than people's opinions. Gail's story, and the other true stories in her book, give hope to all who desire freedom from bondage to their past.

—Jeanne LeMay
Author of *Dear God I'm Desperate: Women Have Issues, God Has Answers*

Gail Porter calls us to a true self rooted in Christ, and that woman is beautiful.

—Lottie K. Hillard, LMHC

Gail Porter's new book, *Living on the Path of Freedom: Leaving Fear of Rejection Behind*, will be your personal GPS to guide you away from fear, rejection, and hopeless living to a new path of liberty, freedom, and the abundant life God meant you to have.

—J. Scott George
Senior pastor, Belle Isle Community Church

Gail's most recent book, *Living on the Path of Freedom: Leaving Fear of Rejection Behind*, tells her story and the stories of ten others who, through no fault of their own, felt the pain of rejection. As a result, they lived according to their beliefs: they were unlovable misfits, deserving mistreatment and abuse. This book reveals the destructive nature of deeds and words that cut deeply and create scars that leave us feeling inadequate and "less than." But that's not the end of the story! We can find hope, healing, and our God-given purpose through our loving Creator.

—Dr. Marvin Terry, DC
Regenerative Wellness of Orlando

LIVING ON
THE PATH OF
FREEDOM

Leaving Fear of Rejection Behind

Live in Freedom!

Dale Porter

LIVING ON THE PATH OF FREEDOM

Leaving Fear of Rejection Behind

GAIL PORTER

Award-winning author of
Will the Real Person Please Stand Up?
Rising Above the Fear of Rejection

Cover design by Carol Tetzlaff
Cover photo by Ulrike Mai
Book design by Colleen Jones

ISBN 978-1-64645-677-2 (Softcover)
ISBN 978-1-64645-679-6 (ePub))

LCCN 2023901301

Printed in the United States of America

Dedication

To the ten people in this book
who courageously shared their stories
because they wanted to give
hope of freedom to others.

For all who are being led by the Spirit of God,
these are sons and daughters of God.
For you have not received a spirit of slavery
leading to fear again, but you have received
a spirit of adoption as sons and daughters
by which we cry out "Abba! Father!"
The Spirit Himself testifies with our
spirit that we are children of God.
Romans 8:14–16 NASB

Contents

Chapter 1

Discovering Truth

*T*he discovery of several linen dresses my mother wore as a small child made me long to uncover more about my own early life.

I'd uncovered many surprising truths about my family while writing my earlier book related to the fear of rejection. Still, I felt a part of my past was missing from my memory.

While I pondered my situation, trying to think of someone who might help me, my good friend Jeanne came to mind. Jeanne had endured an abusive homelife as well as twenty years in an abusive marriage. I admired the steps she had taken to experience healing from her trauma. When God led her to become involved in a ministry of inner healing for women in bondage, I rejoiced with her. God equipped Jeanne with a powerful gift and deep passion to help others.

I knew spending time with Jeanne at her beach condo would help me gain new insights into my past. Reaching for my cell phone, I wandered into my den, where I settled on my brocade sofa to call her. She answered on the first ring.

"Do you have any time to talk this week?" I asked. "It's strange, but even though my book is published, I need to know more about my past.

You're good at uncovering what's inside people, and I need your help."

We scheduled a beach stroll, and it turned into a perfect outing with sunny skies but not hot, and an uncrowded beach. After taking the elevator back to Jeanne's second-floor condo, we enjoyed tuna fish sandwiches and peach tea.

Soon we moved to the elegant cream-colored sofa in Jeanne's living room. Sitting side by side and looking out at the ocean view brought calmness to my heart and soul.

"Are you ready, Gail?"

When I nodded, she said, "I'll ask some questions about your past to get you started. As I always do, I'll invite Jesus to be here with us. He will help you express your thoughts and feelings."

First, Jeanne asked me about my family environment. Then she wanted me to describe my view of our family dynamics. I couldn't remember being a part of anything that had happened around our family's dining room table.

Softly, she asked, "How did that make you feel?"

In my silence, as I thought about her question, deep sobs erupted without warning. With my head bowed, I heard myself say with quivering lips, "I felt sad and lonely. I felt unimportant. And I felt unloved."

Jeanne put her arm around my shoulders.

Time passed. Then I said, "I never knew I felt that way. Whenever difficult emotions bubble up, I push them deep inside."

Hearing myself describe the emotions I felt as a child revealed the truth about my shallow relationship with my parents.

Jeanne explained, "You've uncovered some valuable truths about your family, Gail. When you intentionally delved into details about your family as you wrote your previous book, you reviewed your memories with adult eyes. Today, Jesus helped you look back into your homelife with the eyes of a small child.

"In Hebrews 12:15, God says, 'Watch out that no poisonous root of bitterness grows up to trouble you, corrupting many.' Today, Jesus helped you uncover the bitter root inside you. He brought it into the light so you can begin to deal with the truth of what happened to you. Now you can face reality in God's strength. Let's thank Jesus for what He has done for you."

I will always picture myself sitting with my gifted, compassionate friend who skillfully guided me through our conversation and willingly listened to my childhood sorrow.

Comparing Pictures

After returning home from my time of discovery with Jeanne, I recalled what God had helped me see many years before. From my viewpoint, my parents were kind and good people. They provided a home for my brother and me and took care of all of our daily needs. However, God began to paint a different picture than the one my childhood mind had created.

For the first time, I understood that neither my mother nor my father knew how to create the emotional love connection my brother and I needed and subconsciously longed for.

I couldn't picture their hugs. I don't remember my mom or dad telling me they loved me. I don't recall them showing delight when I strolled into the kitchen in the mornings or ran in from playing with neighborhood children. They never told us "Good job" or "Way to go" to spur us on.

As I continued trying to picture my family, I couldn't recall where the four of us sat at our dining room table. That shook me. I asked my brother, who also had no idea.

I believe I had no picture of us in my memory because nothing happened at our table. We heard no typical questions like, "How was school?" "What did you learn?" "Do you need help with your homework?" Our conversations didn't make us laugh or bind us together as a family. The four of us simply existed in the same house, without a love connection.

When I felt hurt by their words or actions, I never allowed disappointment to show on my face. Instead, I buried each emotion one by one. I didn't allow myself to cry, even in my bedroom.

I longed to know my parents treasured me as their child, but I never received any proof.

Creating Defenses

As I look back on my early years and into my teens, I realize I didn't want people to know me because I didn't think they'd like what they saw. I was quiet and merely listened to people's conversations rather than say anything they might consider unacceptable. I didn't offer my opinion or advice because I'd been laughed at in the past.

I made casual friends at school. I chose only two school friends to confide in. I revealed only facts about my family or personal problems. I never shared my feelings.

My intense search for love and acceptance continued into my adult years. Subconsciously, I participated in what I eventually labeled the great cover-up. To protect myself, I created five defenses.

People-pleasing came first. I tried to become the person I thought others wanted me to be. I carefully observed people's behavior and constantly evaluated my own performance to determine whether I measured up.

In addition, I built a wall. I didn't want to risk anyone getting too close to me and discovering who I was inside. Instead of protection, though, my wall eventually became a castle that imprisoned me.

Sometimes I wore an invisible mask so I wouldn't divulge any of my problems or struggles. Those things would only make me look weak.

Another defense revolved around my unreachable goal of perfection. I thought that if I could be perfect in my job, I would become successful and measure up to my boss's expectations. Each success fueled my desire for greater achievement.

During my first job, I crafted a false identity. My facade made me appear confident and assured, but it only covered deep insecurity and self-doubt.

I thought all these defenses would win me the affirmation and acceptance I deeply desired. In reality, they kept me aloof and isolated from people who might have helped me relax and learn to be myself.

Even my closest friends had no inkling of my cover-up. Since I never shared struggles or problems, everyone thought I had it all together.

Turning Point

I'd lived an aloof life for decades before God unveiled the underlying reason I created all my defenses: fear of rejection. Until then, I didn't know I had that fear. My defenses were supposed to protect me. Instead, they led to a life of deception. After facing the truth, I no longer wanted to exist as the person I thought everyone else wanted me to be. Instead, I wanted to become the person God created me to be.

Without the need to please people, I no longer had to perform to receive approval. God's loving affirmation of me as His daughter was all I needed. I let the bricks crumble from my wall of protection. I was finally free to come out of my hiding place.

I no longer felt motivated to wear a mask to keep people from discovering my problems or struggles. It didn't matter if they thought I was weak. Being weak became a positive step toward allowing people to see the real me.

What a relief to let go of my futile goal of perfection. In its place, I aimed for excellence as a way to show God's work in my life.

I dropped my false identity because God filled me with genuine inner confidence, peace, and joy. Since I no longer needed to pretend, I laughed freely and eagerly joined in group conversations. I relished the chance to be with people and share about our lives. It became easy to tell personal things to close friends who listened, understood, and offered advice. All my friends noticed the difference and welcomed the change.

The Rescue

God overpowered the enemy's schemes that held me in bondage to the fear of rejection. The Lord assured me He loved me just as I was, and He always would. Others may reject me, but God never will.

I consciously stopped believing the enemy and listened to God's voice instead. I already had a personal relationship with Him, but I had allowed fear to rule me instead of relying on the Lord to lead my life. From experience, I knew His voice was the only one I wanted to hear.

My experience with Jeanne and Jesus that day at the beach was part of God's plan to help me dig up emotions I never knew existed. With those last four crucial emotions exposed to the light of Christ, the enemy lost his battle against me. He planned to keep me in captivity, hiding behind a false life, oblivious to the inner destruction that came from believing his lies. He wanted me to keep smiling on the outside so no one would discover my deception. His ultimate goal was to render me powerless to become the woman God had designed me to be.

However, God rescued me from the enemy's power and deceit. No longer bound to the fear of rejection, I lifted my head and walked away. I'd forgotten what freedom looked like: colorful flowers, greenery everywhere, happy smiles of those passing by.

God offered me His hand and guided me to a beautiful path that stretched far into the distance. He looked into my eyes and said, *This is your path of freedom, where you'll become all I have dreamed for you. I will always walk beside you. Whenever you sense fear rising up inside, immediately tell Me. There's no place for fear in your life anymore. You are now a woman of freedom, and I will use you to help set others free.*

Remembering the Journey

After God revealed the truth about my underlying fear of rejection, I thought back on the various seasons of my life. Everywhere I turned, I saw God's love and mercy, which gave me a chance for a full and wonderful life in spite of my fear.

When I was a small child, the absence of emotional love from my parents silently created fear that they would reject me. However, going to church with my parents allowed me to experience God's love. The spiritual seeds planted in my heart led me to take a life-changing step.

One night, during my sophomore year at Oregon State University, I sat with a group of girls at a student meeting sponsored by a Christian campus ministry called Cru (known as Campus Crusade for Christ in those days). The speaker explained that God wanted to have a personal relationship with us.

He said, "God wants to know you personally. He wants to be your Savior and the Lord of your life."

I never knew that before. I always pictured God in heaven and me on earth. Was I worthy to be close to Him?

The speaker offered us a chance to know God personally by thanking Jesus for dying on the cross to pay for our sins and accepting Him as our Savior. Desire flooded my heart. I bowed my head along with my friends and followed the speaker in a prayer of acceptance that began my close relationship with God.

In that moment, my life changed. Later, during the refreshment time, I blurted out to our speaker, "I think I'm on my way." My usual shyness and fear of others dissolved because I knew I belonged to God.

Reading God's Word became more meaningful because He helped me understand the passages. When I joined a girls' Bible study on campus, I met new Christian friends and began to grow spiritually.

New Choices

Ever since entering college, I'd been anxious about my future after graduation. When I learned I could trust God's plan for my life, the uncertainty faded.

Near the end of my junior year, Angie, the woman who had discipled me, asked, "Gail, are you going to join the Cru ministry when you graduate?"

Since I'd dreamed of a career in the business world, I said, "No, I have another plan." Also, I wasn't sure I could succeed as a full-time Christian worker.

The following year, however, God gave me a new desire. I wanted to help others know about Christ as the dedicated Cru staff had done for me. This time, when a different staff woman asked me the same question, my smile blended with joyful tears. "I believe that's what God wants me to do." Her delight in my decision was easy to read.

Before long, I left for my first assignment at Cru's international headquarters in California. Seven years later, I had to make a larger faith decision.

Our HR director, Carolyn Toews, asked me to consider a six-month assignment in Seoul, Korea. She explained I would help foreign delegates who would attend EXPLO 74, a Christian training conference scheduled for August 1974. Carolyn told me to pray about it that weekend.

I'd never been overseas, and I wondered why they'd asked me. What if I couldn't successfully fulfill my assignment there? Typically, I held back from taking risks or going to unknown places. Korea would certainly be an unfamiliar place.

I prayed about this opportunity on Saturday morning, and I was surprised when God tugged at my heart. I sensed He wanted me to say yes because it would expand my world. That morning, the Lord changed my fear and hesitation into faith to accept this six-month venture. I got excited about taking part in this international conference that would draw people from across Korea as well as other countries.

Introduction to Asia

One month later, after sending off our barrels of belongings, our advance team of five women left California and landed in Seoul many hours later. We each joined a different team, but all the teams focused on the foreign delegates.

One of my major jobs was writing a booklet to acquaint foreigners with the city of Seoul. Betty, an American missionary who spoke fluent Korean, offered to assist me. With her valuable input, I completed the booklet. When the books arrived at our office, I was thrilled to see the result of our hard work. Interestingly, that project opened my eyes to my love of writing.

The English newspaper office in Seoul called our office one day. They wanted to interview me for an article highlighting the presence of foreigners in Seoul for EXPLO 74. The thought of being interviewed scared me. I was glad Betty volunteered to go with me.

After a short wait, one of the newspaper staff ushered us across a room filled with multiple wooden desks and workers bustling around. The smile and words of greeting from our young Korean interviewer put me at ease. During the interview, Betty bridged all the Korean-English gaps and filled in necessary information I didn't know.

A fun moment came when the writer summoned a photographer to take my picture to accompany his article. I preserved that memorable newspaper clipping in my keepsake box.

Two months before the EXPLO 74 conference would begin, our team's responsibility shifted to assisting the translators coming from different countries. They set up their electronic equipment in the large tents pitched in a designated area behind the stage, and we served as liaisons.

I prayed I would measure up to the task. In moments of insecurity, my coping mechanisms were useful in overriding my fears. Every time I admitted my fears to God, He assured me He would give me the ability to handle my part of the translators' daily needs.

History is Written

The time finally arrived for the week-long event, which would become the largest training conference in the world at that time. In the daytime, more than 300,000 people gathered for training in various locations throughout Seoul. The evening number swelled to more than one million people who sat on mats in Yoido Plaza, an abandoned air strip. They listened to worshipful music, inspiring messages, and exhilarating challenges to help reach the world for Christ by sharing the gospel in their cities and countries.

The first evening, while people flowed into Yoido Plaza prior to the program, I paused near the front of the towering stage before proceeding to the media tent. I scanned the unending crowd. The women's colorful *kimonos* and men's traditional *hanboks* breathed life into the dull concrete setting.

The sweet, round faces I saw nearby—both old and young people, the majority of whom had traveled long distances, sometimes by foot—did not appear weary. I can still picture their eager expressions. They had come to hear more about Jesus Christ and to learn how to make a spiritual impact in their villages, cities, churches, and families, especially through movements of prayer.

They didn't realize how much they impacted me with their pure and sacrificial desire to serve God with their whole lives, no matter the cost. Their example would light a new calling in my heart.

A Different Plan

Before my six-month stint ended in Korea, Dr. Bailey Marks, director of the Cru ministry in Asia, flew to Seoul for a leadership meeting. There he presented an astonishing invitation.

"Gail, would you move to the Philippines to work in the Central Asia area office after completing your Korea mission?"

I'd never been to the Philippines. It was another unknown place with a high risk of failure for me.

In the end, I said yes to Bailey. God knew I would fall in love with the people. He filled me with a desire to continue serving Him in Asia for what I thought would be a two-year term.

Near the end of August, when my responsibilities with EXPLO 74 ended, I said sad goodbyes to the precious Korean friends I had to leave behind. Tears flowed again as I boarded my flight, but I knew God's next call was the Philippines.

New Ministry Arenas

Three months after my arrival in Manila, our area office team moved to the small mountain town of Baguio. We set up our office in a large rented house.

Part of my assignment was to assist in the annual Asia directors' conferences held in different countries, including Taiwan, Singapore, and Malaysia. Meeting and working with these directors and their staff expanded my expertise, my life experiences, and my circle of friends.

One year, during the conference in Thailand, my boss, Thomas Abraham, announced to the directors, "Gail is available to come to your countries and train your executive assistants."

I froze. I wanted to jump up and shout, "Thomas, you didn't tell me about your plan." I'd never done that kind of training before. The thought of failure took my breath.

To my surprise, the Thailand and India directors asked me to travel to their countries. Once back in Baguio, I scrambled to write a training manual and then scheduled the requested trips.

During the training in both countries, I saw the women's confidence rise. That was all it took for me to embrace this unexpected additional ministry. My fear soon evaporated, replaced by the joy of teaching and seeing these young professional women's lives changed.

Then came a greater commitment. Other country directors, some from closed countries, asked me to come and present multiple-day, citywide training for women who would gather from various cities. I invited my friend and coworker, Ella Crockett, to help present this expanded training. We began extensive communication to discuss the details.

We wondered if we would be able to fulfill the lofty vision of the directors to present valuable training that would impact these executive assistants. Confirmation came when we learned that many of the women had been given additional responsibilities in their offices because of their training.

When my boss, Thomas, first opened those opportunities for me, I doubted my ability. But now I was thrilled that he continued giving me time to train women in addition to assisting him.

A Namesake

Each Friday, our whole office team spread out to various assigned college campuses to share Christ and disciple students. I met Becky at one of those campuses.

A petite freshman with carefully woven braids, Becky sat by herself on a wooden bench in the courtyard. As I approached her, she looked away at first. But when I said, "Hello," and she turned and found a friendly American face, she asked in perfect English, "Would you like to join me?" We quickly exchanged names, and easily began telling each other a few things about ourselves.

During our talk, God created a perfect opportunity for me to share a small booklet, *The Four Spiritual Laws,* that explained how to know Christ personally. Becky readily accepted the chance to pray and trust Jesus as her Savior. In that moment, I never dreamed of the Lord's special plans for Becky.

The next week, Becky brought Luz to our meeting place on campus. Luz was already a Christian, and the three of us enjoyed our weekly Bible study together through the rest of the semester. During those months, I saw Becky's heart for reaching others for Jesus. I felt privileged that God had given me a part in preparing her for what was ahead.

When Becky became a nurse after graduation, her mission field expanded through the medical outreaches she helped organize in various cities in the Philippines. She and her college sweetheart, Jun, eventually married and moved to Manila. Jun became a pastor and together they started a church in their home, always working as a team. When the church family outgrew their house, God provided funds for them to build a church nearby. The church still flourishes.

Becky and Jun named their first daughter Susan Gail, an unexpected thrill for me. Susan Gail and her husband, Carlos, live in Hong Kong with their three adorable children. They both are teachers as well as influencers for Christ in their careers and in their neighborhood.

When I met Becky on campus and introduced her to Jesus, I had no idea she would become a Christian leader and help change lives in many places. Neither did I imagine that our relationship would last a lifetime.

A Time to Leave

Originally, I thought my invitation to work in Baguio, Philippines, involved a two-year term. Near the end of those two years, I prayed and asked God whether I should return for another term. His answer: *Stay there until I tell you to leave.*

That "stay there" turned into twenty-three years. The Philippine national ministry created a local team to take over the operation at the Central Asia area office, and each of us on the American team selected a new assignment with Cru in a different part of the world. My next assignment would take me to Cru's international headquarters in Orlando, Florida.

When our departure day arrived, a friend drove two coworkers and me to the Baguio airport. A handful of Filipino friends waited there to say goodbye. We cried together, not knowing when we would see each other again.

Reluctantly, we turned from our friends and headed toward the compact departure area. As our commuter plane sped down the extremely small runway and lifted us over the valley on its way to Manila, I felt as if someone had ripped out my heart. More tears flowed.

After boarding my flight to the US and settling in my seat, I silently thanked God for the privilege of serving Him in the Philippines for twenty-three years. He had replaced my fear with boldness to walk into unexpected opportunities. Nothing could erase the experiences and memories I had stored in my heart.

Relationships and Marriage

With plenty of time ahead on my overseas flight, I pondered my personal life. In college, I enjoyed two long-term relationships with wonderful and caring young men, one of whom talked to me about marriage. However, with pressure from his family, he returned to his home state for his senior year, which weakened our relationship and ended our thoughts of marriage. Ironically, this shift made it easier for me to follow God's leading to join the Cru ministry after my graduation.

During my seven years in California, I dated several men who loved God and made an impact for Christ in people's lives. But I never sensed God directing me into a permanent relationship with any of them.

In the Philippines, the handful of single American men working at the Asia headquarters kept life interesting and lively for us single

American women. I enjoyed dating a couple of the men, but I didn't feel a deep desire to consider marriage.

Whenever a casual or serious relationship arose but went no further, I simply thought I had not yet found the right man to marry. Now returning to the US at the age of fifty-two, I concluded that God had kept me single to help me fully focus on my ministry without the responsibilities of a wife and mother.

However, after I returned to the States and researched my book about fear of rejection, God revealed the truth about my relationships.

I saw that I never engaged emotionally in my relationships with the men I dated because I was afraid of their rejection if I didn't measure up to their expectations. I designed those invisible defenses to keep me safe from that risk. I wasn't aware that the self-doubt, insecurities, and lack of confidence had caused me to build defenses, but they were only surface symptoms of something deeper.

My underlying fear of rejection prevented me from fully committing to any of those relationships. I thought each breakup was purely circumstantial, never realizing I was the problem. I thought I was in love with each of my boyfriends, but I lived on the surface of all my relationships.

No wonder I didn't cry my heart out when we parted ways. I hadn't engaged enough to feel the deep emotions of love.

After all these thoughts coursed through my mind, a new one emerged. I sensed that God had allowed me the enjoyment of those surface relationships, but His plan all along was for me to remain single. I realized in a new way that my singleness had allowed me unusual freedom and time to embrace a full and vibrant life. I wondered what He had in store for me in my next season.

Timely Transfer

Shifting back to the US and serving at Cru's international headquarters in Orlando opened new ministry opportunities. My greatest joy was joining a team of Cru women in Orlando who wanted to create a life-coaching resource for Christian women. Directed by Susan

Heckmann, our team goal was to help them become influencers in the lives of other Christian women in their countries.

After the whole team brainstormed about the content, three of us wrote *The Significant Woman: Connecting with God, Discovering Your Personal Mission.*

We watched God use this resource to create change in the lives of women in many countries, including Russia, Singapore, and Indonesia. Various countries invited someone on our team to go and present a preview of the resource to the women who had gathered from multiple cities. After being involved in the creation of this resource, I realized God wanted writing to become a major part of my life. Soon He would show me the new steps He wanted me to take.

Shocking Redirection

One day, on a typical sunny Saturday morning in Orlando, I sat sprawled out on my brown wicker chair in the back porch of my condo. There, nestled against the comfy throw pillow, I enjoyed the beauty of the expansive crimson bougainvillea bush climbing the picket fence, the green fan-leaved palm tree perched in a circle of protective ferns, and the symphony of birdsong.

After drinking in new thoughts from my daily devotional book, I reached for my purple journal and poured out my heart to God through written prayers. While writing, I sensed God telling me to let go of my nearly fifty-year career with Cru and begin my own personal ministry in Orlando.

Apprehension surged. My heart pounded as I contemplated this extreme shift from my exciting and fulfilling life to an unknown arena.

Softly, I asked God, "Will anyone accept me as a solo act in Orlando? Will I still have an exciting life?"

Standing at this crossroad of decision, I understood for the first time that God had planned for me to serve with Cru for fifty years, and His plan was near completion. He now called me to leave that safe, familiar road I'd known most of my life and travel on a new path.

I didn't know God's plan for my newest venture, but I knew I wouldn't travel alone. All He wanted me to do was listen for His voice, take the steps He'd set before me, trust Him for my future, and serve Him with my whole heart.

> And now, Israel, what does the LORD your God require of you? He requires only that you fear the LORD your God, and live in a way that pleases him, and love him and serve him with all your heart and soul. (Deuteronomy 10:12)

A New Journey of Freedom

I looked forward to the new adventure of beginning my own personal ministry in Orlando. Now I would have the time to fulfill the passion God had put in my heart to help others recognize their fear of rejection, tear down their defenses, and let go of their fear. Envisioning people learning how to live a life of freedom as God intended excited me.

During a personal retreat at a motel in Cocoa Beach, designed to give me time to contemplate my new calling, God arranged two encounters that would show me a clear picture of my future.

After dropping my bag in my assigned room, I stepped out onto the balcony and breathed the salt air. The sounds of squawking seagulls overhead and squealing children running on the beach filled me with a desire to become part of the scene.

After stepping back inside, I changed into my bathing suit and slipped on my cover-up. After grabbing my beach towel, sunglasses, hat, and camera, I headed for the door.

Outside, I spotted a small bridge leading to the beach. While padding across the wooden slats, I wondered where my footsteps might take me that day.

I spread my towel under one of the small beach umbrellas and lowered myself to the soft sand. Lifting my eyes, I squinted at the aqua water twinkling in the sunlight. A white boat bobbed on the horizon.

To the right stood an old, enchanting wooden pier stretching into the ocean. Surely innumerable people had stood at its railings and dreamed dreams, unleashed secrets to the wind, and received courage to take the next step in their life journey.

Eager to explore, I arose and began my trek. I noticed a solitary, pensive man in swim trunks with a safari hat perched on his head, blocking the Florida sun. He sat on a rise of sand, staring ahead as if mesmerized by the crashing waves. I felt drawn to approach him and ask a rather intrusive question.

"Mind if I take your picture?"

Smiling shyly, he answered, "Sure."

Following the photo shoot, he asked how I'd gotten time off during the week. When he learned about my retirement, he asked, "What are you doing now?"

"I've had time to write another book." The hours spent completing my latest book remained a fresh memory in my mind.

"What's it about?" He looked down at his feet and dragged his toes across the sand.

"Fear of rejection." I wondered what he'd say.

After a pause, he admitted, "Rejection keeps me from saying things, because I want to be perfect."

I sensed pain behind those words. Looking about fifty, he seemed lonely and sad. I wondered what kind of life he'd lived.

He continued, "I'd like to buy your book. I think it would help me."

After giving him my name and explaining how to purchase a copy, I said, "What's your name?"

"I'm Alan. I come to the beach almost every day." He surprised me by revealing seventeen years of sobriety and his regular participation in a local Alcoholics Anonymous group.

"That's wonderful, Alan. God will help you stay sober." *Lord, You know his struggles. Shower him with Your love.*

Alan slowly stood, surprising me with his height and thin build.

His floppy hat had partially blocked his nondescript face while he was seated. Now it allowed a full view of his soft eyes and engaging smile. He thanked me for stopping to talk.

I smiled as I walked away, my excitement soaring. *Perhaps this kind of people connection will become a regular part of my new life.*

That evening, I remembered I had copies of my book in the car. My heart sank. If only I'd remembered. I longed for Alan to learn how he could overcome rejection and stop believing the lie that he needed to be perfect before expressing himself.

I knew he came almost every day, so I searched for him at the same stretch of beach. No Alan.

Another Unexpected Meeting

Three months later, I stayed overnight at the same Cocoa Beach motel where I'd met Alan. Before returning to Orlando, I decided to look for him. I had no guarantees, but I wanted to try.

I slipped into my car and chose the winding path that paralleled the beach. My heart's desire became an audible prayer: "God, You know exactly where Alan is. Please lead me to him."

Sensing I might be near my destination, I parked my car on a side street and grabbed the book. As I wandered toward the beach, I encountered a tall, thin woman with her adorable dog.

She noticed my book and asked, "What are you reading?"

Holding it up, I smiled. "It happens to be a book I wrote."

Upon reading the title, she gasped and threw her arms around me.

Stunned, but wanting to acknowledge her obvious trauma, I said, "You've faced rejection too."

"All my life," she gloomily replied as her sad story tumbled out. After offering her name and asking for mine, she mentioned her AA group.

Could it be?

"Teresa, several months ago I met a man named Alan on this beach. He wanted to read my book because it's about rejection. He said he's part of an AA group here. Do you happen to know him?"

"Tall, skinny?"

"Yes!" I felt like jumping for joy.

"He attends often and our group meets tonight. I'll give him your book."

Teresa bent down to pet her dog. Looking up, she exclaimed, "I can't believe this!"

"Me either!" I marveled at God's goodness. "Teresa, let's take some pictures!"

After arriving in Orlando, I texted our photos. Tears gushed down my face as I read her joyful reply: "You blessed me today . . . God with skin."

First Alan and then Teresa. The bond between the three of us became a symbol of how God had changed me. I'd lived a regimented, guarded, predictable life, full of deep-seated results of my fear of rejection. However, through those God-ordained encounters, I experienced the thrill of loving people deeply and genuinely and connecting with them easily. My new freedom had truly begun.

Enjoy the upcoming chapters about people like you and me who got to see God's amazing healing up close and personal.

Rejection crashed into each life and thrust most of them into a troubled, dark, hopeless existence without love. Two of them experienced blatant rejection at the ages of three and four.

Out of their darkness came a ray of light and love from our heavenly Father. He penetrated the darkness created by the enemy who wanted to rule their lives through fear of rejection.

You will see the unique ways God rescued them and brought redemption, freedom, and transformation. God used counselors and pastors, along with those gifted with the ability to bring about inner healing, and other compassionate people who came alongside those wounded people and helped free them from their bondage.

None of them will forget the trauma that shaped the person they became, but the memory of those experiences will no longer overpower them. God brought their buried emotions and experiences to His light and took away the enemy's power to constantly remind them of their past and reinforce shame and fear of rejection.

I pray that my story and the other stories will become stepping stones for you to move forward, destroy the defenses you've built, come out of your hiding place, and leave your fear of rejection behind.

You can escape captivity, experience freedom, and become the person God intended you to be. God created a path of freedom for you that showcases the person you are inside. The enemy wants to keep you bound to your fear; God wants to set you free.

No matter what you've experienced—deep trauma, endless struggles, overwhelming circumstances, debilitating fear—God will use your past to give hope to others.

You are no longer a slave to the enemy. You are God's adopted child. He cherishes you and delights in you.

> For all who are being led by the Spirit of God, these are sons and daughters of God. For you have not received a spirit of slavery leading to fear again, but you have received a spirit of adoption as sons and daughters by which we cry out, "Abba! Father!" The Spirit Himself testifies with our spirit that we are children of God. (Romans 8:14–16 NASB)

God wants you to live with joy on your path of freedom. He will give you strength to accomplish His plans for you. He will pick you up when you falter, give you rest when you become weary, and celebrate each milestone on your new journey. Best of all, He loves you and will be with you forever.

My Personal Prayer:

_____

_____

_____

_____

_____

_____

_____

_____

_____

_____

_____

Bible Memory Verse:

For the LORD your God is living among you. He is a mighty savior. He will take delight in you with gladness. With his love, he will calm all your fears. He will rejoice over you with joyful songs. (Zephaniah 3:17)

Chapter Challenge:

- Write out some Scripture verses confirming that God loves you, delights in you, and will always be with you. Praise God by praying one of those Scriptures back to Him.

_____

_____

_____

_____

_____

_____

_____

_____

- Can you think of a time when you were fearful because of what someone might think of you? Have you ever been afraid to step into a new opportunity because you thought you might fail? Did you overcome your fear? How did God help you? Journal about your experience and ask God to help you face your fear in a different way next time. Meditate on this truth: "For God has not given us a spirit of fear and timidity, but of power, love, and self-discipline" (2 Timothy 1:7).

_____

_____

_____

_____

_____

_____

- If you are aware of any negative, accusatory thoughts in your mind, give those thoughts to God. They are from the enemy, not God. Meditate on Ephesians 6:10–18, which explains the spiritual armor God has given you. Each day, verbally announce the different parts of His armor you are putting on, which will enable you to stand firm against the enemy's schemes.

Chapter 2

Rewritten Stories
Enid Walker Orr

God surprised my widowed friend Enid when He led her on a path to remarriage.

You may have met Enid in my first book, *Will the Real Person Please Stand Up: Rising Above the Fear of Rejection.* In the last line of her story, she said, "The inner stories I told myself all those years—that I wasn't lovable and, therefore, people would leave me—are being rewritten."

Indeed, God began to rewrite Enid's inner stories. But before I talk about the new happenings in her life, here is a review of my first conversation with Enid about her fear of rejection.

A Casual Dinner

Brisk spring breezes brushed our faces as Enid and I slid into wrought-iron chairs on the patio of a favorite restaurant. After submitting our order and showing our latest family pictures, we leaned forward, eager for unhurried conversation after a few months apart.

Seemingly oblivious to the street noise from the nearby intersection, Enid introduced the first question. "How's your book project coming along?"

"Since I have more time to write these days, I'm making progress.

It's been easy to collect stories because rejection is a common fear."

"Well, let me tell you my story of rejection."

I never imagined Enid would feel rejected. She engages with people easily, speaks to groups with confidence, and attracts admiration from everyone who meets her.

Enid explained, "I always fear my friends will suddenly not want to be with me. Recently, I remembered a kindergarten memory for the first time. I had two special girl friends in my class. Before every recess, we ran to the playground together. One day, they went without me. When I ran over to them, one girl said to me, 'We're both sick, so you can't play with us.' I knew they no longer wanted to be my friends.

"I started crying. My teacher came over to find out what was wrong, and I told her what had happened. She turned to the other students around us. 'Who wants to play with Enid?'

"I was afraid no one would answer. But Andrew said, 'I want to play with Enid.' Andrew became my rescuer that day."

"That's the event that triggered your fear, isn't it, Enid?"

"I realize that now. The same kind of thing happened when I attended an integrated high school. Soon a white classmate and I became best friends. We were together a lot at school, and one day she invited me home. We had a lot of fun talking and playing together.

"The next day, as soon as my friend saw me, she said, 'My mother told me I can't be friends with you anymore.' Our friendship ended that day."

I couldn't imagine how Enid felt in that moment. All I could think to say was, "I'm sorry that happened to you."

"It didn't stop there," she said. "Tyrone and I met in one of our college classes, and eventually we started going steady. During Christmas break, we both went home. I thought he would call me, but he didn't.

"When I returned to the campus and saw him, all he said was, 'Over Christmas, my old girlfriend and I got back together. That's why I didn't call you.' Another rejection."

I reached across the table to place my hand on hers. "Such painful times. Do you still experience your fear of rejection?"

"I still have lingering questions. Will people welcome me? At times I feel the same emotions as I had during my school days."

"Emotions stemming from childhood can rise up without warning," I said. "You've recognized some of your early triggers, though, and that's a good beginning for rising above your fears."

Our evening ended with smiles and hugs.

A Turning Point

I'll always remember that first conversation with Enid during our dinner date in Orlando. It was that conversation that prompted me to include her rejection story in the book I was writing at that time.

After receiving the first draft of her story, she suggested a Zoom call. I loved connecting with her that way. It gave me a chance to see her smile, detect her tears, and hear her laughter. I enjoyed the experience of "sitting" in her den and watching her golden retriever wander in and out.

Her first comment was, "I'd like you to include another college experience that changed my perspective on my fear of rejection."

I saw excitement in her eyes.

"Remember Andrew, my rescuer on the kindergarten playground?" Her face brightened as she recalled her little friend's kindness.

Enid continued, "I discovered another rescuer while attending Spelman College. Some of my girlfriends invited me to a special student event on campus. That night, we strolled to the gathering, glad for a reason to get out of our dorm rooms.

"A woman welcomed the students and then began talking to the crowd about God. At the end of her presentation, she asked people to come forward if they wanted to pray.

"I waited to talk with her. I told her I definitely wanted to know God, but I didn't see how that was possible because I'd done things that displeased Him. She showed me 1 John 1:9: 'If we confess our sins, He is faithful and righteous to forgive us our sins and to cleanse us from all unrighteousness.' With her help, I understood that Jesus's death and resurrection made forgiveness possible. I prayed for forgiveness and accepted Jesus as my Savior and Lord. That night, He became my permanent Rescuer."

My eyes misted with tears, her experience reminding me of my own. "How wonderful. Jesus also became my permanent Rescuer in college."

Then Enid told me an immediate result of her commitment to the Lord. "My experience that night happened shortly before my college boyfriend rejected me. My Christian friends wondered how I would respond to my heartbreak as a new Christian.

"This time I took my rejection and broken heart to Jesus. He reminded me of God's love and promise in Hebrews 13:5: 'I will never desert you, nor will I ever forsake you.' My college boyfriend deserted me, but I knew Jesus never would. That truth helped to heal my heart. My friends were amazed."

"That's a beautiful example, Enid. I'm eager to add that to your story."

Enid held up her colorful journal. "I love recording my thoughts each time Jesus overpowers my fear of rejection by reminding me He will rescue me in every situation."

The Next Episode

As Enid predicted, God began rewriting her story after *Will the Real Person Please Stand Up?* released in 2018. Unexpectedly, God asked me to write a companion book four years later.

As the content for the new book began to evolve, I called Enid. "God has led me to write another book that will focus on living on the path of freedom. I'd love to include your continuing story."

"Sure. You'll know how to weave my old and new stories together. Now it's a matter of finding a time to talk."

New Discoveries

Finally, we captured a mutual day to do another Zoom call. After chatting for a while, I asked Enid, "Did our conversation over dinner several years ago help you better understand your fear of rejection?"

"Ironically, before we talked that evening, I had to read a book for a class. While answering questions relating to my life, I realized that the early events I told you about were still in my memory and had affected my perception of situations and relationships."

Another perfect timing by God. "I have another question for you, Enid. How did you meet your husband?"

"I met JT through the college boyfriend who'd rejected me. The three of us were already friends before my boyfriend and I started dating. After we broke up, I was a bit hesitant to become more than friends with JT for fear of losing him too. However, JT and I continued our friendship, which developed into a romantic relationship."

Enid paused and smiled as if she were recounting their early days. "JT and I met Rodney and Cortina when we were engaged couples. The four of us were in the process of becoming full-time staff members of Cru. We took a marriage class together and went on double dates. Both marriages took place that summer. Cru assigned us to different locations but we kept in touch."

Parenting

"JT and I loved being parents to our two sons and three daughters. Never a dull moment in our household. We two couples supported each other in everything. This became a special blessing when God took JT to heaven in 2004 after his courageous battle with leukemia. It was a devastating time, and I felt lost."

"I wish I could have known JT. Obviously, everyone admired him. What a deep loss for you, Enid."

Sorrow flooded her face. "I still miss his presence. Before JT's death, our family moved to Springfield, VA, just outside Washington,

DC, where JT began serving on the pastoral staff team at a church. That church family gave us amazing support after JT's death.

"Several years later, I began working remotely as part of Cru's Significant Woman Team based in Orlando. Through my involvement, I lived out my purpose to help change women's lives. The Significant Woman life-coaching resource paved the way for me to lead women's events, both in my church and others."

In addition to the loss of JT, Enid's son and daughter-in-law lost their first child after only a few hours of life. The double tragedy changed their lives, especially Enid's, since she had to face all the emotions of the loss without JT.

God gave John-Mark and Meg additional children, and Enid enjoys being a grandmother. She held up a picture of her granddaughter.

"She's adorable. I admire your family for being there for each other during those times of deep disappointments."

Just then Enid's phone rang, and she excused herself.

The Surprise

When Enid returned, I was ready with my next question. "I've heard about a new relationship in your life. Sounds as if God is rewriting your story."

She laughed. "You know how JT and I were close friends with Rodney and Cortina. After JT died, Rodney and his wife encouraged me in my new life. When Cortina died in 2017, I called Rodney to express my sadness for his loss. We continued exchanging ministry prayer letters and prayed for each other.

"Rodney had become a professor at Dallas Theological Seminary in Dallas, Texas. During his sabbatical from teaching, he served in China, teaching English academic writing to engineering students."

She went on to explain that during Rodney's sabbatical in China, he realized he didn't want to be single for the rest of his life. As he prayed about his desire, Enid's name and face came to mind. He decided that, when he came back to the US, he would look for an opportunity to spend time with her.

Enid's viewpoint: "It was sweet of him to think about me from China."

"Sounds like a pleasant development," I said with a grin.

Enid laughed at my not-so-subtle inquiry. "When Rodney got home, he emailed and asked to meet me for coffee when he was in my area. Unfortunately, my schedule was packed that week. I had no available time. We decided to talk by phone. Both of us were nervous, but our friendship picked up right away once we heard each other's voices."

"So it all began with that first connection," I said with a giggle. "Did Rodney return to the States?"

"Yes. Not to Washington, but we were in touch every day."

"I can't wait to hear about the next step."

An Important Announcement

A few months later, Enid sent me an unexpected text. "Gail, call me. I have something to tell you."

I immediately phoned her. "Enid, here I am. What's your news?"

"Rodney and I are engaged! I'm sending a picture now."

I gazed at Enid's tall, handsome fiancé and Enid's beaming face, her hand resting on Rodney's chest to show off her beautiful engagement ring. "Enid, I'm so happy for the two of you. How did this happen?"

"As we began to spend a lot of time together, we fell in love. We both wanted a companion, and we believe our loving relationship is God's plan for fulfilling our personal desires."

I asked Enid, "When Rodney started showing interest in you, did you worry about how everything would work out?"

"No, I had a long walk with Jesus while I was a single mother, and that brought contentment. My life was full of friends, meaningful work, and great relationships with my five adult kids. I enjoyed the thought of having someone in my life, but I was happy either way."

"What gave you courage to say yes to Rodney's proposal? At any point, did you think about your painful experiences with rejection and wonder if this new relationship would last?"

"It helped that we'd known each other for years," Enid said. "We both served with Cru, we had mutual friends, and we shared the same hopes and dreams. God's faithfulness was obvious long before Rodney proposed, because God had provided the necessary connections to bring the two of us together. That assures me that Rodney and I will love each other faithfully throughout the rest of our lives."

With the blessing of their children, Enid and Rodney married three months later.

Wisdom for Relationships

God helped Enid overcome fear of rejection and gave her confidence to enter into marriage. After three traumatic rejections in her growing-up years, God brought Rodney into her life. I saw a sharp contrast between then and now. Rodney chose Enid to be his bride and vowed never to leave her.

A year had passed, and I decided to drive to a nearby park and call Enid. After finding a bench a safe distance from the squeals of children on the merry-go-round and swings, I pulled out my phone.

After only one ring, I heard Enid's sweet voice, and I asked if she had a moment to talk.

"This is a perfect time to take my dog, Ralph, for a walk in the neighborhood. I'll call you back in a few minutes."

Soon my phone buzzed. We both were eager for family updates, so that came first. Then she asked about my book.

"Well, you know me," I said. "I'm always pondering the effects of fear of rejection in our daily lives. Do you have any words of wisdom?"

After a pause, her answer came. "I think I still have a small layer of fear inside me. Sometimes, talking to myself helps me separate my fear from reality. Often, it's the same emotion I felt when JT died of cancer and I was left alone. That same fear rose up when John-Mark and Meg lost their newborn son, Jacob."

"God understood your fear during that traumatic time in your life, Enid."

Just then I heard her dog yelping.

"Ralph saw one of his favorite dog friends and is bouncing and twirling in front of him. I'm going to sit on this bench for a few minutes and let them play.

"I've learned some new things lately, not only related to Rodney and me as a married couple, but also about friends.

"Letting go of fear is not a onetime decision. With each new experience, I must choose to turn loose of fear and trust God. I cringe when thinking of the friendships and adventures I would have missed if I had let my fear of rejection stop me. I realized I had allowed my fear of rejection to hold me back from establishing close, authentic relationships. I'm thankful that God has shown me how to engage and be more real with my friends."

Enid paused as if contemplating her next words. "I try to be wise in choosing my friends. When I meet someone new, I always decide how much I'll tell them about myself and my past until I get to know them better. As I grow in my trust, I become comfortable sharing more of who I am."

I shifted on my bench and glanced at the laughing children. Enid had imparted crucial input for creating more authentic relationships. As I listened to her wise advice, I realized that God had increased my trust in other people and shown me how to become more genuine in my conversations.

"Thanks for all your valuable and meaningful advice, Enid. What you shared helped me realize I've grown in my own ability to establish more open and honest relationships. I also appreciate your perspective on meeting new friends."

Enid immediately responded. "We often meet people who are different than we are and who have different ways of relating to others. Some will reject me and some won't. But as I've grown older, my reaction to rejection has changed. Now I have my relationship with Jesus as my Savior and friend, and He provides the anchor I need when I feel rejected. I know the lengths Jesus went to in securing me as His friend, and this gives me much satisfaction. No matter what others may say or do to me, Jesus will never leave me nor forsake me."

Reality in Marriage

"I've made some new discoveries since meeting Rodney. I can't talk so freely about these things at home, so let me get Ralph walking again, and I'll tell you."

Just then shouts of the children on the merry-go-round erupted. Enid waited for the noise to subside.

"Husbands and wives can never completely meet each other's needs. Rodney and I have different values and methods of relating to each other. Sometimes, when those differences crop up, I feel that old twinge of rejection. But God has given Rodney and me the tools we need to work through those differences and move toward each other again."

"Enid, you should write a marriage book." I sensed her amusement.

"I don't know about that, but I've discovered that the same process takes place in my relationships with my children and now Rodney's children. Building relationships on love and not letting fear overpower my love is a continuous learning process. Most of the time, working toward freedom is an exciting adventure. It can still be scary when Rodney and I don't think alike, but I trust God with my relationship with him and others. This all takes time and practice. But we've been practicing getting to know people all our lives. I've read that from the time we're born, we all hunger for human touch and human faces."

That was an interesting fact to ponder. Human touch and human smiles certainly lift me above any problems or insecurities I may feel in that moment. As I glanced at my watch, I realized I needed to let Enid get back to her other responsibilities and maybe even give Rodney a kiss.

"I assume you must be close to home by now, so I'll ask one last question before we say goodbye. God has certainly rewritten your story through meeting and marrying Rodney, hasn't He?"

Enid gave a beautiful explanation. "Rodney is a wonderful part of my life—a surprise gift from God. I'm still amazed at the way He poured love into my life when I least expected it. Rather than rejecting me, Rodney chose me for his wife. We enjoy learning and growing together as a married couple."

Enid added, "As wonderful as our marriage is, my relationship with Jesus is my true anchor. My heart is tethered to Him as my best lifelong, eternal friend. He gives me hope, dispels my fear of rejection, soothes my pain, and shows me how to move forward in my relationships with family and friends. His love and strength give me the courage I need to keep walking in freedom."

> This hope is a strong and trustworthy anchor for our souls.
> It leads us through the curtain into God's inner sanctuary.
> (Hebrews 6:19)

When Jesus became Enid's permanent Rescuer from her fear of rejection, He also became her anchor for life. Then He provided a wonderful partner for her here on earth.

I marvel at the way God gave Enid a personal relationship with Jesus at the appointed time. Also, I'm amazed at the connections God created to bring Enid and Rodney together so they could enjoy a loving relationship in the second half of their lives. Their love story reminds me of a cherished passage:

> LORD, You are my God; I will exalt You, I will give thanks to Your name; for You have worked wonders, plans formed long ago, with perfect faithfulness. (Isaiah 25:1 NASB)

Recently, Enid flew to Orlando for a meeting. Before her return flight, we spent an hour together in a restaurant near the airport, enjoying a salmon dinner and exchanging news.

Enid also related important discoveries she and Rodney had made recently. "While talking with our counselor, we learned that childhood experiences affected our behavior and responses. When we began processing those experiences separately and personally and giving them to God, our marriage changed. We enjoy each other much more now because we no longer need to be cautious about what we say, and we're more accepting of each other."

I saw the difference in her face. The stress and tension were gone. In fact, she was radiant.

After dropping Enid off at the airport, I pondered the way her discoveries had led to a change of behavior and a smoother and more enjoyable relationship with Rodney. I saw their new freedom as evidence that Enid had conquered the fear of rejection that once bound her to a behavior of hesitancy. Now she is free to be the joyful, relaxed, and engaging person she truly is. Transformation took place in Enid's life when God rewrote her inner stories of rejection.

My Personal Prayer:

_____

_____

_____

_____

_____

_____

_____

_____

_____

_____

Bible Memory Verse:

You didn't choose me. I chose you. I appointed you to go
and produce lasting fruit, so that the Father will give you
whatever you ask for, using my name. (John 15:16)

Chapter Challenge:

- When and how did God rescue you from your fear of rejection? What kind of person were you then, and what are you like now? Journal your thoughts so you can refer to them later.

  _____

  _____

  _____

  _____

  _____

  _____

- God loves you and intentionally chose you. How has this knowledge changed the way you think about yourself? List two changes you've observed.

  _____

  _____

  _____

  _____

  _____

- God promises never to leave you nor forsake you. How has this knowledge altered your thinking about your future? Share this question with a close friend and interact together.

  _____

  _____

  _____

  _____

- If you are married, review Enid's advice in this story and in the podcast with her daughter-in-law (see link below). Choose one suggestion you want to apply to your marriage.

_____

_____

_____

_____

_____

_____

_____

Enid's daughter-in-law, Meg Walker, interviewed her on her podcast called *Teach Me about Grace*. For your enjoyment, here is the link: https://teachmeaboutgrace.buzzsprout.com.

Chapter 3

From Victim to Victor
Thomas Carter

"*I* wish you didn't look like your mother."

These frightening words from a sullen, angry, disengaged father had infiltrated Thomas's young mind. He had no inkling of the devastation that lay ahead for him.

Only recently had my friend Thomas revealed some of the trauma he'd faced growing up. One day he asked a surprising question: "I want to write my life story. Will you help me?"

I quickly agreed, because I wanted to help Thomas fulfill his dream. We decided to meet at a nearby library, where I reserved a conference room.

It was a sterile room, without any decor on the walls, but it provided our desired privacy. We chose seats across from each other at the narrow table. Rather than intimidate Thomas with my open computer and limit our eye contact, I chose to take notes by hand. I reached into my bag, and pulled out my new yellow lined pad.

Thomas had brought with him a small notebook and a shiny red ballpoint pen.

Neither of us could predict how our meeting would flow, but we knew God was there with us. After we each took sips from our water bottles, I prayed that God would give Thomas courage to speak and me the ability to listen well and generate readable notes.

Without hesitation, Thomas began relating his startling story. "As an eight-year-old boy, I heard my parents arguing frequently, but I never observed violence between them. My father's unpredictable anger toward me often sent me racing to the farthest corner of the house. I cowered there, waiting for my older sister, Bonnie, to rescue me."

I learned that Thomas's mother, another protector from his father's wrath, built a codependent relationship with Thomas that would continue the rest of her life. In Thomas's words, "We were inseparable. We went everywhere together."

Unbearable Loss

"Then tragedy struck," Thomas continued. "When I was only ten years old, my mother died in a head-on collision. She and her sister were heading back from a department store, where she'd exchanged my new shoes for a larger size. My aunt survived the tremendous impact; my mother did not."

Thomas and his older sister, Bonnie, were in school when the police came to the house to tell his father about the accident. One of the aunts called the school and asked them to send the children home. Neither Thomas nor Bonnie knew the reason.

"When Bonnie and I arrived home and heard the news, we clung to each other and cried. Our father didn't know how to provide comfort for us in the midst of his own heartache, so he asked one of the nearby aunts to come and take care of us. Then he left the house for several days."

I couldn't imagine facing the loss of the only person who showed him love. "Thomas, I'm so sorry. You must have felt abandoned, even though your aunts were around."

Thomas reached for his red pen, rolling it back and forth in his palm.

"I felt alone in the world when my father left. Now I understand he couldn't bear the sadness of staying in our house without my mom.

I found out later that he was nearby, making sure our needs were met, and helping my aunts prepare for the funeral. When everything was set, Aunt Lisa took me to the service. I saw my dad, but we exchanged no words or hugs. Still, having him there made me feel less alone.

"While I sat in that sad, dark place, guilt consumed me. My young mind whispered, *It's your fault. If she hadn't been exchanging your shoes, she would be alive.*"

Sadness upon sadness unfolded when his uncle Leonard picked Thomas up and forced him to look at his mother in the casket.

"The woman inside looked nothing like my mother," Thomas said. "That experience left an indelible, distorted image in my mind and robbed my memory of the sweet face of my mother, who loved me and protected me all my life."

Thomas's agonizing separation from the comfort of his mother set the stage for his intense craving for love.

After the funeral service, Thomas and his father returned home. His father showed no emotion toward him, speaking few meaningful words to his son. His frequent bursts of anger left Thomas afraid to approach him, even to talk. The silence fueled Thomas's fear of rejection.

"That was when you needed your father the most, Thomas. How sad."

Later, when Bonnie gave in to Aunt Lisa's pleas and went to live with her to help take care of her three-year-old daughter, Brittany, Thomas felt even more alone and unloved.

Upheaval from the Familiar

"A few weeks after my mother's death, my father decided we'd move from West Virginia to Florida. Uncle Robert, who'd moved to Florida earlier and established a combination garage and gas station, asked the other uncles in West Virginia to relocate and go into business with him.

"My dad and I traveled south, leaving Bonnie behind at Aunt Lisa's home so my sister could continue caring for Brittany and going to school.

"The other two aunts and uncles settled in the same vicinity as my dad and me. The move seemed good for my father, who was a skilled mechanic."

Looking at Thomas's dark-blue eyes in that quiet room, I tried to read what was going on in his head. "Sounds as if your aunts and uncles settled into life easily, but what about you?"

I saw embarrassment on Thomas's face as the truth poured out. "Some of my relatives were teachers in my West Virginia grade school. I floundered in my classes, because of my inability to read well. I should have been held back, but out of sympathy for the loss of my mother, they kept advancing me to the next level. When I arrived in Florida, I was already far behind academically, and I had difficulty understanding the new, more advanced curriculum. When I had to repeat seventh grade, I was ashamed but tried to stuff my feelings inside."

"I'm sorry, Thomas, for all you faced in your new environment."

"Even worse, my dad started drinking heavily to drown his sorrow. As an adult, I realized my mother's death had shown my father how much he loved her, and he couldn't bear her absence. Undoubtedly, he thought the move to Florida would help. But it didn't. I still feared my father, and I missed Bonnie's encouragement and protection."

I imagined Bonnie's absence created a large void in Thomas's life. He had no one on his side.

"Then my dad began making trips to West Virginia. After one visit, he returned with a woman, announcing, 'We're married, and this is your new mom.' The woman brought her thirteen-year-old son with her, while her other son and daughter stayed behind in West Virginia."

Thomas had somehow survived yet another upheaval. "How did you feel about this sudden, drastic change?"

Thomas hesitated, apparently deliberating how to explain his feelings. I waited. Finally, he said, "When this new person suddenly became my stepmother, I felt even more distant from my father. I never got along with my stepmother or her son. Her main focus became drinking with my dad.

"Soon my stepmother began hitting me and abusing me physically and verbally. My father never believed my stories about her. Then one day he came home unexpectedly and saw his wife throw a skillet at me, injuring my knee."

Although his father said nothing, the evidence declared the truth. That evening, after a lot of yelling in the back bedroom, his father walked into the living room, where Thomas sat on the floor, playing with his stepmother's cat.

"I'm taking her to back to West Virginia in the morning," his dad said. "We're getting a divorce."

Vindication descended on his young heart. But his father's favor was short lived.

Invasion

It felt as if Thomas and I needed a break, so we wandered down the hall and spotted a backroom where we bought soft drinks from what looked like a twenty-year-old vending machine.

When we returned to the unadorned but private meeting space and set our drinks on the table, Thomas continued. "During my junior high years, I dreaded coming home because of my father's anger and heavy drinking. Before going in, I always peeked through our front window to gauge my dad's mood.

"One day after school, I went through this ritual. This time, my father's recliner pointed toward the window, and he stared at me. I jumped back in horror then tiptoed inside.

"I crept down the hallway and slowly peered around the corner into the living room. Dad's loud voice bombarded me. 'You remind me so much of your mother. I wish I didn't have to see you. Get out of my face.'"

Thomas sped to his room and waited, heart pounding. The words crushed Thomas's spirit and heightened his sense of vulnerability.

Imprisoned in his room with nothing to eat when evening approached, he decided to go to sleep. He slept until he was jolted awake by the presence of his father lying in bed beside him.

I looked at Thomas's sorrowful face. He whispered, "That was when the molestation began. It continued for two years. I hate to admit it, but I enjoyed it because it won my father's attention and affection, which I had longed for all my life."

That's such a sad scenario, but common. His father pulled him into abnormal and destructive behavior, but Thomas's starving heart couldn't resist the chance to be close to him. This childhood invasion would remain in Thomas's heart and affect his behavior and choices throughout his life.

Rescue in the Wings

One evening, while visiting his friend Mike, Thomas confided in him. Shocked, Mike assured him he didn't have that kind of relationship with his own father. At that point, Thomas realized his homelife was not normal. Guilt filled his heart, but he didn't know how to stop his father from molesting him.

God had not forgotten Thomas. He knew the pain in the boy's victimized soul. God set in motion a plan to set Thomas free from his father's abuse.

"Each day, my father drove from the office garage to the bank to deposit the day's earnings," Thomas told me. "As protection, he always carried a pistol. Until one day.

"I spotted the gun at home and made a decision. The next time he came close to me, I was going to shoot him."

I gasped. Burying my face in my hands, all I could do was moan as I pictured a squad car taking away this innocent young boy.

I looked up at Thomas's face, crumpled with remembrance. "I can only imagine your desperation in that moment. You had no one to protect you."

"That was how I felt. The next day, my cousin Kenny called and asked for a ride home in my car after school. When I sauntered into their dining room, Kenny's mother, Aunt Joan, evidently recognized the outline of the pistol in my jacket pocket.

"'Please tell me that's a BB pistol,' she screeched at me.

"'No, it's Dad's gun, and I'm going to kill him with it.'

"'Look at me, Thomas. I know something is wrong with your dad. We haven't known what to do about the situation. But give me the gun.'

"After she pleaded with me for a while, I finally gave in and handed it to her.

"'Stay right here,' Aunt Joan said. 'I'm going to your house.'

"I remember the droop in my shoulders as my aunt stormed out the door. I told Kenny. 'I'm dead. My dad's going to kill me.'

"When Aunt Joan returned, she explained, 'I confronted your dad and gave him his gun back. I don't believe he's going to molest you again.'

"But I was afraid to go home, so I asked to stay at Aunt Joan's house. In the morning, I went home. I thought Dad would be at work, and I could avoid him until the evening. Instead, he sat in the kitchen with a half-filled coffee mug, his shoulders sloped and a lifeless expression on his face.

"He looked me in the eyes and said, 'I'm going to work.' From then on, he came home each evening at dinnertime, but he never took advantage of me again."

I breathed a sigh of relief. God had miraculously broken Thomas's father's power over him. God also kept Thomas from making a decision that would have destroyed his life.

A Look at the Future

"After two more years of high school and then trade school, I moved into an apartment. One of my friends introduced me to her roommate, Paula."

Thomas was attracted to beautiful Paula. Sadly, despite the trauma his father had caused, and being full of guilt, Thomas slid into a sexual relationship with Paula. She became pregnant right away.

"To make things right, I decided to marry her. When her mother discovered my plan, she cautioned me against it because of the way she saw Paula treat other men. However, I was determined. We named our daughter Terri, and I eventually adopted Paula's three-year-old son, Daniel."

After eight years, Paula had an affair and filed for divorce. Their marriage came to an end.

Out on his own and still searching for love, Thomas met some gay men. He adopted the gay lifestyle because he got so much attention. He and Jay became partners and lived together for eight years. Thomas's lifestyle choice broke Bonnie's heart, but out of love for her brother, she tried her best to accept his life.

"By that time, Dad had married another woman. This stepmother was kind to me and had good instincts. She told me, 'Your father is trying to be better.'

"Eventually, my dad and stepmother moved back to West Virginia, where they still had family and friends. The first time I visited them, I felt more comfortable and safe in that environment than I ever had.

"The day before I returned to Florida, I walked into the living room where my dad sat reading the newspaper. He looked up at me and said, 'I didn't always treat you right, but I love you.'"

I felt like crying when Thomas described that tender moment. "That's amazing, Thomas. How did you feel when he said that to you?"

"That day would be the first and only time I heard those words of love from my dad. I will always treasure them. But anger for his past abuse still coiled inside me."

Dealing with the Past

The next year, Thomas's stepmother called him with sad news. His father had been diagnosed with cancer and was in the hospital. He wasn't doing well.

"My aunts, uncles, and I immediately drove fifteen hours to the West Virginia hospital. My sister, Bonnie, met us in the lobby.

"My first glimpse of my dad took my breath. I'd never seen him in that condition. Fortunately, he knew me and we were able to talk briefly.

"Dad asked for Bonnie. She came into his room, but unable to bear the heartache of seeing him, she left the room and returned only to say goodbye."

While in town following his father's death, Thomas visited his father's grave several times. Nothing had been resolved between them, and anger ate him up inside.

"On my last visit to my father's grave, I stood before the tombstone and yelled at him. I ranted and raved as my anger spilled out.

"Hearing the commotion, a guard at the small cemetery approached me and asked if I was all right. I told him I only needed to sort things out and release some anger."

I felt relieved that Thomas had the chance to vent. "Releasing your anger and the emotions inside you surely began the healing process."

"Yes, it did. When I returned to my aunt's home, I told her what happened at the cemetery. She laid her hand on my arm and said, 'You needed to do that.'

"I knew it was unhealthy to hold on to my anger and resentment, and I asked God to forgive me. God helped me realize my father was a broken person. His own parents had never shown him love, leaving him without the capacity to love me and our family.

"For the first time in my life, I felt free of anger. God's forgiveness helped me recognize my father's desire to provide a home and food for us, even though he couldn't love me. A picture popped into my mind: my father's scribbled note on a napkin—the one that always appeared whenever he left for the weekend. The message always said *I'll be back on Monday*. A fifty-dollar bill lay next to his note.

"Shortly after my visit to Dad's bedside in West Virginia, I learned that he had called his nephew, Donald, and asked him to come to the hospital. Immediately, Donald went and began talking to him about spiritual things. In a soft voice Donald told me, 'I led your dad to faith, Thomas. He received Jesus and I could tell he was very sincere.'

"My dad died that night." Thomas looked at me across the table, his eyes still full of wonder. "After hearing this wonderful news from Donald, God reminded me of the day I had said to myself, 'I'm glad Mom knew Jesus and she's in heaven. I wish I could see my father there too.'"

"And now you will! What a moving story, Thomas."

The Rest of the Story

As a young boy, Thomas had gone to church with his mother and knew about Jesus, but because of his destructive decisions, he sometimes wondered if God still loved him. Very soon Thomas would discover the unconditional love of God.

The uncovering began when his sister, Bonnie, bought Bibles for Thomas and Jay for Christmas. Thomas explained, "Jay threw his Bible away and hid mine. I believe he knew it would lead to the end of our relationship.

"I started reading my Bible. I was looking for something new, because homosexuality was empty. Jay knew something had changed. Through an unbelievable decision on his part, he forged my signature on a large check that had mistakenly arrived at our apartment. Then he tried to deposit it into my account. The bank found the check suspicious and froze my account during the investigation. Jay wound up in jail, which brought our relationship to an end ten years ago.

"God knew I never could leave Jay on my own. When the time was right, God provided a way of escape. I sensed Him saying to me, 'I did this for you because I love you.' My certainty of His love gave me courage for the future."

"God showed up for you, didn't He?"

"Yes. His love was very clear, and He began to show me the right steps to take."

I prayed God would bring people into Thomas's life who could help him heal from the trauma that had continued to influence his decisions.

A New Life

"After my relationship with Jay ended, I packed up everything I owned and started a new life, including a job with Stanley Steemer," Thomas said. "I searched for a counselor who could help me sort out my life. I happened to find one who'd lived a gay lifestyle until God set her free. Out of all the counselors in town, God led me to someone who would understand my longing for love, my loneliness, and my new desire to walk on a different path."

The counselor invited Thomas to her church. There he met Darrell and Dorothy, who'd each lived the gay lifestyle but had walked away several years before. They'd eventually crossed paths and ended up sharing their stories. After falling in love and getting married, they had begun a discipleship ministry specifically designed for those coming out of the gay lifestyle.

"I joined their classes and experienced God's forgiveness. I gave my life to Christ and discovered the true and unconditional love of God. As I faithfully attended the weekly classes, I grew in my faith and began living in God's grace.

"Darrell and Dorothy moved to Texas a few years later, but we kept in touch. Then I received a phone call from Dorothy, who told me Darrell had died from AIDS. I had to face this devastating loss of a true friend, who loved me and had introduced me to the Savior."

New Leading

Darrell and Dorothy helped to change Thomas's life. God brought them together so Thomas could find Christ and become their disciple. Through their influence, Thomas had gotten used to asking God for His next step. When he did, God led him to his current church.

"My new church supported an organization that provided thirty days of housing to addicted men from the streets. Eleven houses in the same neighborhood offer safe harbor. The men get a chance to become clean as they attend our church for spiritual nurturing and fellowship. They come to Bible studies at the center, receive leads for jobs, and learn how to live a Christ-centered life that will fortify them in the real world."

Thomas went on. "My heart immediately engaged with the thought of helping these men. For several years, I discipled the guys in the program. As one man became strong enough to leave that temporary home, a new one took his place.

"Another mission group outside my church heard about my involvement with these men and invited me to become part of their ministry. Their mission is similar: show Jesus to people on the streets, teach them about Christ, help them turn from their addiction, and show them how to follow Him on a new path. Those on the streets usually have sad and destructive lives. They find it difficult to hope for any other kind of life.

"I remember one night when some friends and I walked the streets where many homeless people congregated. We were ready and willing to talk to them about Jesus. The three of us felt prompted to stop that night and talk with a prostitute named Connie. God had prepared her heart."

Connie later told Thomas that she had been praying for someone to come, but didn't believe it would happen. When she saw Thomas walking toward her, she whispered to herself, "Is this the man?"

"That night, the three of us told Connie how much Jesus loved her and that He wanted her to follow Him on a different path than she was living. When we explained more, Connie expressed her desire to ask Jesus into her heart. When she lifted her head from praying, she shocked us by saying, 'I want to walk off these streets and follow Jesus.'

"We said to her, 'We'll help you. Meet us here at nine in the morning, and we'll pick you up.'"

Thomas and the couple knew about Priscilla, a woman who opened her home to prostitutes, since she had been a prostitute herself. Thomas called Priscilla that night and discovered she had room for Connie in her home.

"The next morning the three of us reached our destination and spotted Connie. A smile spread across her face as she lifted her bag and flung herself into the car. Her rescuers had arrived."

Connie stayed with Priscilla for a few months. When a better home became available up north, Priscilla explained the details to her and then arranged and paid for Connie's flight. Priscilla and Connie kept in touch, and each time they talked, Priscilla let Thomas know the latest about Connie.

Then Thomas told me about a surprising phone call from Connie. "She said, 'You told me God loves me, but how could He, after all the horrible things I've done?'

"'Ask Him to show you a sign,' I said."

Not long after that conversation, Thomas heard from Connie again. "This time, she said, 'I'm in a phone booth, looking down the street. A big sign says *Jesus loves you*. I think I got my sign!'"

"That's amazing, Thomas! You were God's instrument. Connie wanted to walk off the streets and follow Jesus, and you helped her. Because of you, Connie will walk with Jesus on a beautiful new journey. He'll be there to pick her up and reinforce His love whenever she needs it."

A New Man

"I thank God every day that He transformed my life," Thomas said. "He's willing to use me, even after all I've been through."

I paused from taking notes, marveling at the changes in his life. Quickly, I began writing again when I realized Thomas was expressing words that showed the depth of his relationship with His Father God:

- God is the Father I never had.
- I trust God, and He trusts me.
- When God sends someone to me or prompts me to do something, I know He trusts me.
- The Lord uses my imperfect life to show others that imperfection is not a problem. God takes the imperfect and makes it perfect.
- God takes something negative and makes it positive.
- The Lord's work brings redemption.
- My earthly father always complained I was too sensitive and emotional. Now I realize God created me this way because I will be sensitive to the people He brings to me.
- My Father loves me, connects with me, and never holds things against me.

- All my life, I've been starving for the things God has given me.
- God poured into my life all the love I needed to become a free person. Whenever I listen to needy people, pray for them, help them find Christ, or show them how to grow in their new faith, my heart fills with peace, contentment, and thanksgiving.

> Therefore if anyone is in Christ, this person is a new creation; the old things passed away; behold, new things have come. (2 Corinthians 5:17 NASB)

As a victim of other people's warped desires, Thomas felt burdened by the fear of rejection. But God brought His chosen people into Thomas's life and began to transform him into a victor. With the support of godly people, Thomas has dealt with his past and maintained his devotion and pure heart in order to serve the Lord. Knowing the enemy will always remind him of his past and bring guilt, Thomas learned to give each accusation to God and lean on Him for deliverance.

As a victor, Thomas experiences God's power to lead people to Jesus, so they can become followers and live a life of freedom as he does.

We are in a spiritual battle today. The enemy of God fuels our fear of rejection because he doesn't want us to come out of our hiding places and live in freedom. He whispers lies in our ears about who we are, and we can easily begin to believe what we hear.

God's Word confirms the intensity of our enemy:

> Stay alert! Watch out for your great enemy, the devil. He prowls around like a roaring lion, looking for someone to devour. (1 Peter 5:8)

Our all-powerful God knows all about the enemy's schemes. We are not in this battle alone. The Lord fights our battles for us. He has given us His mighty armor to protect us from the enemy's tactics and help us stand firm in His power.

Ephesians 6:10–18 is a beautiful picture of the ways we can prepare for spiritual battle each day:

> A final word: Be strong in the Lord and in his mighty power. Put on all of God's armor so that you will be able to stand firm against all strategies of the devil. For we are not fighting against flesh-and-blood enemies, but against evil rulers and authorities of the unseen world, against mighty powers in this dark world, and against evil spirits in the heavenly places.
>
> Therefore, put on every piece of God's armor so you will be able to resist the enemy in the time of evil. Then after the battle you will still be standing firm.
>
> Stand your ground, putting on the belt of truth and the body armor of God's righteousness. For shoes, put on the peace that comes from the good news so that you will be fully prepared. In addition to all of these, hold up the shield of faith to stop the fiery arrows of the devil. Put on salvation as your helmet, and take the sword of the Spirit, which is the word of God.
>
> Pray in the Spirit at all times and on every occasion. Stay alert and be persistent in your prayers for all believers everywhere.

It is not enough to put on our spiritual armor only one time. Each day we must outfit ourselves with God's full protection.

No matter what you have faced in your life, you can become a victor like Thomas by walking in God's power and protection every day.

My Personal Prayer:

_____

_____

_____

_____

_____

_____

_____

_____

_____

_____

Bible Memory Verse:

Be on guard. Stand firm in the faith. Be courageous. Be strong.
(1 Corinthians 16:13)

Chapter Challenge:

- It is important to put on your spiritual armor every day so you can stand firm against the enemy. Put on the helmet of salvation, the breastplate of righteousness, the belt of truth, the shoes of the gospel of peace, the shield of faith, the sword of the Spirit, and the undergarment of prayer. What might be an easy daily reminder for you to put on this armor?

_____

_____

_____

_____

_____

_____

- If you do not have a regular prayer partner, think of a friend you could invite to pray with you. Praying for each other's needs during the week will create a valuable prayer covering for both of you.

- Pause and praise God for an answered prayer today. Praise helps you enter into the presence of God and keeps you focused on Him rather than your circumstances.

_____

_____

_____

_____

_____

_____

Chapter 4

Filling Empty Spaces
Gretchen Young

"My fear of rejection caused me to make a heartbreaking decision." I tilted my head and studied my best friend as we sat in a cozy booth in the back corner of Perkins, eating chicken salad. I had envisioned a carefree conversation. Perhaps not.

Gretchen and I always looked forward to hearing about each other's ups and downs. The statement she had just made, however, alerted me to a surprising low point in her life.

I searched Gretchen's face. "You've never had a problem with rejection."

"I never realized it before." Gretchen set down her fork. "Only this week God reminded me of a decision I had made about Ronald fifteen years ago when he was near death. God revealed to me that I'd let my fear of rejection determine my action that day."

Gretchen's son, Ronald, was her life, special to all of us. I'd never imagined anything going awry with him. Yet he had gone through a tragic death because of his unwise decisions.

Life-Altering Choices

Gretchen looked at me with hesitancy. "Gail, thank you for going through Ronald's unexpected journey with me. You know a lot that happened to my family during that sad time, but today I want to tell you the full story of what I went through. Some details will be familiar; others will shock you.

"You knew Ronald had been a mortgage broker, and he lost his job during the recession of 2006. It was downhill from there. He was distressed but diligently searched for a job.

"Ronald and his third wife, Lori, had been married for two years when Ronald began taking prescription drugs to ease the pain of his migraines. Jack and I knew about the prescription drugs, but we soon noticed a change in his behavior.

"We tried to intervene a couple of times, but Ronald wasn't willing to get help. One day I called my ex-husband, Sal, and he flew in from California to try to persuade Ronald to go into rehab. When we arrived at Ronald's house, Lori said he didn't want to go, and she stopped the intervention."

Gretchen's sad eyes and solemn face reflected the despair she must have felt at that time.

"I resented Lori in that moment. However, when God revealed my fear of rejection last week, I realized that Lori had faced the same dilemma. She made her destructive decision because she was trying to please everyone. Lori didn't want Ronald, or any of the family, to look down on her as the bad person who had forced Ronald to do something he didn't want to do. As with me, her fear of rejection overpowered her ability to think clearly about what was best for Ronald."

"It seems like everything had stalled."

"Fortunately, we began to see a glimmer of hope that our attempts at intervention had impacted Ronald. He faced the truth that he was addicted to prescription drugs. He said he wanted to stop, especially since he was looking for a job.

"He visited his doctor and asked him to discontinue his prescriptions. The doctor decided to discontinue the drugs altogether, rather than weaning him off. Ronald struggled with this method because of the pain of withdrawal, so he supplemented other prescription drugs he bought from a fellow he knew who sold them illegally."

Until now, Gretchen hadn't shared with me those additional details about Ronald's addiction. I felt sad I hadn't known, yet we all were praying for Ronald.

A Glimmer of Hope

Gretchen placed her fork down and adjusted her napkin. She waved at our server and held up her coffee cup.

After slowly drinking a few sips of her hot coffee, she took a deep breath. "Near the first of December, while I was meeting with a group of women, Ronald called my cell. He asked me to pray for the job interview he'd scheduled with a mortgage company for that afternoon. I assured him I would. After relaying the news to the women seated around the table, we all prayed for Ronald's interview.

"I was so happy when Ronald called me with good news—that was when the mortgage company hired him as a broker."

I nodded, remembering that day.

Gretchen continued. "They scheduled him to begin working the first part of January 2008. Ronald looked forward to this chance for a new beginning."

I had seen it as a wonderful new beginning for him, too.

"Gail, I have more to say, but let's take a quick break."

I welcomed the chance for us to walk away for a few moments. I couldn't imagine how difficult it was for Gretchen to relive those experiences.

We slowly walked back to our seats. Gretchen reached for her glass and took a long drink of water. "Gail, I want to tell you what happened later in December that year. I can't remember what I've already told you, so I'll give you the complete story.

"On December 22, I had breakfast with Ronald and his son, Ronnie, who would have been eleven then. You remember Ronnie lived with Ronald, but his nine-year-old, Carolyn, lived with his ex-wife Deb, who had adopted Carolyn while they were still married. After breakfast, Ronald took Ronnie to Port Charlotte, about two hours from Orlando, to spend the Christmas holiday with Deb and Carolyn."

Looking pensive, Gretchen said. "I found out later that on December 23, Ronald and Lori talked at home about taking a trip, to soften his disappointment in not being able to see his two children on Christmas.

"Earlier that evening, Ronald had picked up another supply of his prescription drugs from the same fellow he had contacted before. When he admitted this to Lori, she became angry. She had chosen to side with him and block an earlier intervention attempt by his grandfather, but now she realized rehab was the only answer. She pleaded with Ronald to change his mind. He declined.

"Lori called me and said she had told Ronald, 'If you don't give up the drugs, I'm going to leave.' Nothing was resolved between them, so Lori moved into her mom's house that night."

Gretchen went on to explain that on December 24, she invited Ronald to spend Christmas with her and her husband, Jack. However, Ronald was too upset about Lori moving out. He said he wanted to be alone.

"I dreaded the outcome of Ronald being by himself at their house, but didn't know what else to say.

"On December 26, when Lori returned to the house, she and Ronald got into another argument. He took off on his motorcycle."

I was visiting family on the West Coast at that time, when Gretchen called to say Ronald and Lori had argued and Ronald had left on his motorcycle. I was afraid about Ronald's drugs and his anger and kept asking God to keep him safe.

The Unraveling

Because of Ronald's erratic and frightening behavior, Lori contacted the police and put the Baker Act into effect. With this in place, officers can apprehend a person who has exhibited behavior that indicates mental illness, if the officer believes they may harm themselves or others.

"Lori called me late that night to tell me the police found Ronald and escorted him to a psychiatric facility. I felt relieved to know Ronald was off the streets. But our worries weren't over.

"The facility placed Ronald on suicide watch, which meant someone would check on him every fifteen minutes. But then, contrary to protocol for someone on suicide watch, they placed him in a room with another man."

I moaned, while wondering how the facility would have risked violating that crucial rule.

"The next morning Ronald called me. 'Mom, you've got to get me out of here.' He told me to send Jack. I told him to calm down and that Jack and I would come over later. I stalled to allow Lori time to complete an injunction at the courthouse that would prevent Ronald from returning to their house."

I didn't know how complicated things had become.

"Perhaps after our conversation, Ronald felt even more desperate. From what we pieced together from investigative reports, he asked his roommate to help him. Since that man had been incarcerated many times and knew how to work the system, he showed Ronald how to use a sheet to fake a suicide attempt. According to the plan, a staff member would find Ronald in time to transport him to the hospital for a complete checkup. Knowing Ronald," Gretchen said, "he probably thought once he was in the hospital, he would find a way to escape."

I shivered as I tried to picture this scary scene.

"Since the staff made rounds every fifteen minutes, Ronald's roommate knew when to complete the setup so someone would find him in time. But later, we discovered that the man somehow managed to leave the room before the scheduled rounds so no one could blame him for helping Ronald.

"Unfortunately, the employee did not follow the rounds schedule that night. When Ronald was found, he was unconscious and soon lapsed into a coma. The facility called for an ambulance to take him to the hospital, then they informed Lori.

"I had talked to Ronald only a couple of hours before Lori called me, saying he was in the hospital. I couldn't comprehend what had happened."

Devastating News

I remembered Gretchen calling me to tell me Ronald was in the hospital and she and Jack were headed there to stay with him. My emotions began rolling inside of me.

Gretchen said, "Lori and I were both shocked with the news from the hospital, but we knew we had to call the rest of the family. Since Ronald's children were still at Deb's house for the Christmas holiday, we purposely delayed telling them about their father's condition.

"When Jack and I walked into Ronald's room, I'll never forget my heart stopping when I saw his pale face.

"Early the next morning, the other adults arrived at the hospital. We gathered around Ronald's bed, hoping somehow he would know we were there. We still couldn't believe this was happening and tried our best to console one another."

Listening to Gretchen, I envisioned the despair they must have felt in that hospital room.

"As we stood there, the medical team came in to tell us they had determined there was no hope of recovery for Ronald. Our hearts shattered. I prayed out loud, 'God, please help us and give us a miracle.'

"The staff assured us they knew Ronald was an organ donor. They told us they would perform the procedure after we'd said our last good-byes.

"We began talking together about Ronald's children. We all felt it would not be good for them to come to the hospital and see their father unconscious, so we decided to ask Deb to bring the children to Lori's house so we could spend time with them there.

"After visiting with the children, we all planned to return to the hospital to say our last goodbyes. Our family had prayed for a miracle, but we had to let Ronald go.

"Before going to Lori's house, we all stood by his bedside again, tears gushing down our faces. We could hardly bear the thought of saying our last goodbyes. I informed the staff we would be leaving but would return in a few hours."

A Silent Battle

Gretchen said, "As I sat in Lori's living room, I wrestled with conflicting desires. I wanted to be there to comfort Ronnie and Carolyn when they arrived, but I also desperately wanted to be in Ronald's hospital room keeping vigil.

"Self-doubts began to sway me. *What will my family think of me if I leave before the children arrive? They're depending on me to help comfort the children. I'm afraid they'll feel like I don't care about their sadness.*

"My intense desire to avoid displeasing my family won the battle. Laying my grieving, wounded heart aside, I decided to stay with the family and help console the children."

I couldn't imagine how Gretchen withstood the pressure of making that decision in that moment.

"Before the children arrived at Lori's home, my cell phone lit up with a call from the hospital. I stepped into one of the bedrooms and accepted the call.

"A woman identifying herself as hospital medical staff said, 'We're sorry, but there's been a complication. We won't be able to perform the organ procedure for Ronald, so we are ready to remove his artificial respirator now. Can you come?' I told her I needed to talk to my family."

Gretchen said she stumbled into the living room and blurted out,

"That was the hospital. They can't harvest his organs, and they're ready to remove the ventilator. They need to know if we can come."

Her family decided since they had already said their goodbyes earlier, and the children hadn't yet arrived, they should give the hospital permission to go ahead.

Gretchen's eyes filled with tears. "I wanted to leave immediately to make sure I saw Ronald's sweet face one more time before they removed the ventilator. However, once again, I gave in to my self-centered fear. I called the hospital with the answer and then joined the family in the living room.

"We all cried together again, but the rest of them will never know the depth of my sorrow about missing my last chance to see my son.

"As grief flooded my soul, I crumpled onto the living room couch. I never spoke to anyone about my inner struggle and the regret I would carry forever.

"Nothing could change the tragedy of what had happened to Ronald in the psychiatric facility," she said softly. "Some restitution came to us when a complete police investigation took place after the incident, due to suspicion of criminal neglect."

Gretchen explained that the facility had been found guilty of placing Ronald with a roommate while he was on suicide watch. The police wanted to question the roommate because he was the only person who had access to Ronald and could have shown him how to stage a suicide. The police had his name, but they couldn't locate him. They concluded that the facility knew they were at fault and had covered up by getting rid of the man.

Ronald's wife sued the facility and won a settlement, but no amount of money could relieve the sorrow.

The Way of Forgiveness

I sat motionless in my booth, overcome with shock after hearing the complete story about Ronald. I had already shed many tears with Gretchen over the loss of Ronald, but the new tears that coursed down my cheeks represented a new sadness that my friend had to endure fifteen years of sorrow and regret all by herself.

Seeing my tears, Gretchen reached for my hand from across the table. "Gail, I believe God chose this week to reveal my fear that people will reject me if I don't please them. Now I see how that kind of fear causes people to speak and act the way they believe other people want them to in order to be accepted.

"That day, as Ronald lay in that hospital bed, I cared more about fitting in with my family's plan, and not disappointing them, than laying my fear aside and doing what my heart longed to do: see Ronald one more time.

"I asked God's forgiveness for giving in to my fear and making my wrong decision fifteen years ago. He forgave me and assured me I'd been a good mother to Ronald.

"His forgiveness brought release to my troubled heart. For the first time, I felt relief."

My own heart lifted. "Thanks, Gretchen, for telling me about your intimate conversation with God. It's amazing how the discovery of your fear of rejection led you to find freedom through God's forgiveness. I'm thrilled for you."

We gathered our things and walked to Gretchen's car, where I gave her a long hug. That day we became heart-and-soul friends because of the deep and personal things we shared with each other.

New Revelations from God

One evening, several months later, Gretchen called me with surprising news. "Gail, I want to tell you about some other memories that have surfaced since our discussion about rejection. Shockingly, all these memories relate to my fear of rejection."

In my own experience, God hadn't uncovered all my emotions at once. He had His own timing for letting each buried emotion rise to the surface. Like Gretchen, all of them related to my fear of rejection. I was eager to hear what God had done for Gretchen.

"I wish you didn't have to face those buried emotions," I said, "but this is part of your healing."

"I'm glad I can talk about these things with you, Gail. It helps me process.

"I'll begin by telling you about my marriage to Sal. We knew each other in high school and rode the same bus. We reconnected when we were nineteen, and he was in the navy at Cape Canaveral.

"Sal and I dated for nine months and enjoyed mutual interests. Since he was on a ship and gone a lot, we tried to do fun things while he was in town.

"In 1968, we decided to get married, and we bought our first house in Titusville, Florida. Ronald was born in April 1969. We were thrilled to have him in our lives.

"After two more moves within the state, we built a beautiful home on Merritt Island, which overlooked the Indian River. Its completion was a special delight, because we both loved the water. I enjoyed decorating and making our home beautiful and inviting.

"A couple of years later, Sal received a job offer in south Florida. He wanted to take it, so I agreed to give up my job at Kennedy Space Center. I was excited about starting a new business and a new life. It was a sad day, though, when I had to walk away from my beautiful home on the island."

A few more pieces of her life fell into place for me. "I remember when you showed me that home during one of our weekend getaways. I didn't realize the significance for you. It must have been sad to see it again."

"It's become less sad over the years, but it will always represent a part of my life I lost."

Gretchen continued, "A couple of years after we moved, Sal suddenly spun into a midlife crisis. He seemed restless. One day he announced to me, 'I'm not in love anymore. I want to experience more in life.'

"I should have suspected something had changed, because he hadn't shown any interest in my new photography business. My world stopped. Life had been great and then suddenly it wasn't. A deep and profound feeling of rejection descended over me. I was no longer wanted. We simply separated—he by choice and I by default. The divorce came a few years later."

The Uprooting

Trying to mask my anger, I asked, "So what happened when Sal uprooted you?"

"Sal declared he was staying in the house. The only place I could think of to go was Orlando, where my sister Julie lived. Feeling numb and displaced, I tried to gain some stability there, but because of the stress and heartache, I became anorexic.

"I closed out my photography business before I left south Florida. Now, six months later, I felt strong enough to look for a job. I began working at the Clinique counter at Dillard's department store. Eventually, I was promoted to manager.

"All of us on the team became close friends. I had noticed that Kate, one of the young women, was always joyful, in spite of her difficult homelife. No matter what kind of customers she encountered, she always had a smile on her face."

I could only imagine how much Kate brightened their work environment.

"One day, I asked Kate how she was happy and joyful every day. She said it was because she had Jesus in her heart. She explained to me how I could know Jesus personally.

"Then she said, 'I'd like to invite you to my church.'

"The next Sunday, I drove to her church. Everyone was friendly, and I felt surprisingly at ease. At the end of the service, the pastor explained how we could know Jesus as our Savior. I thought I was a Christian because I had gone to church my whole life. But Kate had told me how to know Jesus personally, so I knew I wanted to pray."

I loved to see God's perfect timing play out in her life.

"When the pastor invited us to come to the altar to pray, I immediately left my seat and walked to the front. Kate came down quickly from the choir loft and joined me as I prayed along with the pastor. I felt peace I'd never experienced before. That peace helped me begin to put hurtful things in my life behind me.

"Kate was thrilled to be a part of my new decision to become a Christian. From then on, we talked a lot about Jesus at work. Valerie, who worked at a different cosmetic counter across the aisle, came over often to talk with us."

I anticipated what would come next.

"Valerie always asked, 'What are you talking about?' Soon we told her about Jesus. Kate invited her to church, and she received Christ too."

"God was surely at work at your counter, Gretchen. It's exciting to hear about the effect Kate had on all of you."

"We also got to know a police officer named Jack, who had worked at Dillard's for a long time and knew everyone. His job was to patrol the store, so he stopped by our counter often. He particularly liked talking with me. He even starting using Clinique products."

And most likely Jack provided good protection for the ladies as they walked to their cars in the evening.

A New Horizon

"Since we knew Jack well, our group decided to invite him to join us for dinner one night. However, we all canceled our plan at the last minute, but I forgot to tell Jack, and he went to the restaurant. He stills jokes that I stood him up on our first date."

"So this is how your romance started!"

"Yes. Soon he asked me out for a real dinner. That first date led to other dinners and spending time together on our days off. We enjoyed seeing movies and taking day trips to nearby cities. Jack introduced me to his mother and eventually to his brother and sister, all of whom lived in Gainesville. They were easy to know, and I quickly felt close to them."

Meeting his family meant it was serious.

"Jack and I enjoyed a close and comfortable relationship for six years. During that time, we talked about marriage off and on, but nothing materialized. Finally, I announced, 'If you're not interested in getting married, I'm going to start dating other men.'

"Everything changed. That Christmas, Jack proposed and gave me a beautiful diamond ring."

Gretchen had introduced me to Jack. I knew they had dated for a long time, and I remember thinking to myself, "It's about time."

"We married in April 2000. After buying a house in Orlando, we settled into our new married life. We especially enjoyed our nearby church. Jack became my rock, the one I leaned on when traumatic events began to happen in my family."

Family Issues

I knew our conversation would now turn to Gretchen's son, Ronald, and her grandson, Ronnie—and those were sad stories. I took a deep breath and silently prayed that God would protect her emotionally and give her courage to express herself openly as part of her healing.

Taking a short break, we spoke briefly of more trivial matters. Then I asked, "Tell me more about Ronald. He was your life, wasn't he?"

"Absolutely. I loved Ronald with all my heart. He married Krissy when he was twenty. They were thrilled with the arrival of their son, Ronnie. The baby added joy to my life, too, making me a new grandmother. I thought things were going well for them, but when Ronnie was only two years old, they divorced.

"I thought Krissy would have full custody of Ronnie and I would seldom see him. That thought devastated me. However, Krissy decided to give up custody of Ronnie so his life would not be divided. This was a great sacrifice for Krissy but a blessing to me."

A mixed blessing, for sure.

"When Ronald remarried, he and his new wife, Deb, moved with little Ronnie to Texas, where Deb had a job lined up. Ronald knew he could easily find a job as a mortgage broker. After a couple of years, they had Carolyn. Ronnie loved being a big brother. We wished the family lived closer, but they sent pictures frequently, and we visited them occasionally.

"Next, they moved to Kentucky. I thought the family would stay together, but after five years, they divorced. They both moved back to Florida—Deb to Port Charlotte and Ronald to Orlando."

"That must have disappointed you, Gretchen, especially since it separated the children."

"The only good thing was Ronald and Deb shared custody of the children. During the school year, Carolyn lived with her mom and Ronnie with his dad. During the summer months, the children took turns being together at each parent's home.

"This arrangement enabled us to see both of our grandchildren whenever Carolyn came to Orlando to spend time with her dad. We often had sleepovers at our home with Carolyn and Ronnie, and sometimes only with Ronnie when Carolyn wasn't in town.

"Two years later, Ronald married Lori. Sometimes I worried about all the upheaval Ronnie had been through, but he seemed to settle into life with his dad and stepmother. He did well in school and made new friends."

A New Era

"Thanks, Gretchen, for giving me all the details about Ronald and his children during those earlier years. By the time I moved to Orlando and met you, I was in my early fifties and Ronald and Lori were already married. I'm glad for the times we went to their home, especially when both Ronnie and Carolyn were there."

"Jack and I were very glad that Ronald and the family lived nearby. At this point, life was good, but you know everything that happened after that."

My heart sank as I recalled those memories. "I still cry when I think about Ronald's death. You suffered a great loss, and your heartache will never go away. I'm glad God knows how to comfort you each time you think about Ronald."

"God was always by my side. I would have given anything if I could have protected Ronald from his destructive choices."

Holding back tears, I said, "I'm sure every mother who has lost a son through wrong choices feels the same way. I'm glad you found a good support group."

"My church's GriefShare group allowed me to interact with people who understood my loss."

I had always been so happy that she'd found this network of grief recovery support groups that provides healing from the hurt of losing a loved one.

"I was blessed to have the opportunity to lead two GriefShare groups the following year. God softened my own grief while I helped other suffering people."

Broken Communication

I hesitated to ask Gretchen about Ronnie because she was facing a major heartbreak as his grandmother. Finally, I said, "Tell me about your relationship with Ronnie before he went into the Marines, like his grandfather Sal."

"Ronnie and I were very close. I have wonderful memories of our times while he was growing up as well as the years following his dad's death. He lived with Lori, so we had meals there together sometimes. I brought him to our home, where he enjoyed the pool and especially the meals we grilled outside.

"Once he was of age and joined the Marines, he was on an aircraft carrier, gone for long stretches. We still texted each other and sent pictures when we could. I always looked forward to his next return, when I'd get to see his handsome face and hug him—and then listen to the details of his latest military adventure.

"I never expected anything to come between us. However, Ronnie didn't call me before he left to go back on duty after one of our visits, which was very unusual. Shockingly, his silence continued without explanation."

How did Gretchen bear this sorrow? "I'm so sad you haven't found a way to connect with Ronnie and find out what has caused the distance between you."

"I can't even explain the hurt in my heart. Ronnie's stepmom, Lori, chose not to tell me when he was coming to Orlando for a visit. I felt helpless to change the situation. My heart ached to see Ronnie."

Because of the unusual details surrounding Ronald's death, including medical negligence, the whole family was traumatized. Relationships became strained even back then.

Gretchen said, "I could understand Ronnie's heartache from the loss of his father, but I didn't understand why he pulled away and stopped talking to me, after we'd created a way to stay in touch even though he was in the Marines. His abrupt, abnormal behavior made me think someone had told him lies about me, and he thought I was somehow responsible for his father's death."

"Gretchen, I can't fathom anyone being that cruel to you or to Ronnie."

"Over the years, I hoped our relationship would heal, but that hasn't happened.

"My latest sorrow was finding out, after the fact, that Ronnie had come to Orlando for a visit. His grandfather, Sal, traveled from California to see him. The supreme rejection piercing my heart is the picture of Sal and Ronnie in a bear hug. His stepmother, Lori, posted it on social media."

My hand flew to my heart. I couldn't even imagine how deeply that hurt Gretchen.

"If I didn't know Jesus as my Savior and Lord, my despair and feelings of rejection would have overpowered me. Instead, God gave me strength to keep going and not give up. I choose to believe God will help Ronnie know the truth and will restore our wonderful relationship one day."

"I pray for that, too, Gretchen, and I'll never stop."

Gift of Redemption

In the midst of our busy lives, Gretchen and I found another window of time to share stories and to process together. One afternoon, we perched at a small wooden table outside the Coffee for the Soul café, one of our new finds. The young staff, all from Venezuela, wore bright smiles and loved serving us delicious soups and entrées created from their home country recipes.

After tasting my chicken stew, I said to Gretchen, "It's been fun to watch you develop a closer relationship with Carolyn. Ronald would be pleased. And now Alice has filled your life with love, acceptance, tons of hugs, and lots of laughter, hasn't she? I love seeing her sweet smile and bouncy curls when you post pictures."

"Little Alice lights up my life. We enjoy creative activities together, especially painting. Even though I'm her great-grandmother, I feel young around her."

Carolyn and Edward live close enough to Gretchen and Jack for them to travel back and forth to visit. Soon Alice will have a little brother—another grandchild for Gretchen to love.

Touching Lives

Gretchen then introduced another subject. "Do you recall the times when we facilitated women's conferences together—even overseas—and taught weekly Bible studies at church?"

"You were in your element."

"In those days," Gretchen said, "God kept bringing needy people across our path so we could encourage them, pray with them, and give them hope. Recently, I realized I've gotten away from that kind of ministry. I miss it, and I've asked God to restore my passion to help other people know Jesus and grow in their faith.

"Within days, God answered my prayer. And it involves Evelyn. You knew she was visiting, but I didn't have a chance to tell you that she became very ill and was hospitalized last week.

"During one of my visits to the hospital, I told her about Jesus. The next time, I explained about salvation, and she accepted Jesus as her Savior. We easily talked about heaven. She told me that no matter what happens, she will be with God."

I felt like standing up and clapping. My greatest joy comes when I know someone has embraced Jesus. "Gretchen, what a beautiful, divine answer to your prayer."

"God is amazing. He kept Evelyn here in Orlando so I could show her the path to eternal life, because she entered hospice care when she returned to Gainesville."

We both rejoiced that Evelyn is headed to her eternal life.

"Gail, I'm still leading the weekly Zoom calls with my group of women. I'm glad we are currently studying your book, because it gives me a way to help these women overcome their fear of rejection and live freely as the women God wants them to be."

"I'm proud of you for touching many lives, Gretchen."

"During all my sad times, God stayed by my side. Now He has restored my passion and reminded me of His purpose for my life. He keeps opening new doors for me to help women see themselves as God sees them and be engaged in His purpose for them.

"Even though I've experienced rejection throughout my life, God filled the empty spaces in my heart. He helped me overcome my fear so I could look beyond myself and enjoy a life full of joy."

> You will make known to me the way of life; in Your presence is fullness of joy; in Your right hand there are pleasures forever. (Psalm 16:11 NASB)

Gretchen had many heartbreaks in her life, especially involving her family. As she said in her story, "If I didn't know Jesus as my Savior and Lord, my despair and feelings of rejection would have overpowered me."

After feeling rejected in many different situations, Gretchen experienced redemption. The Lord filled the empty spaces of loss and feelings of rejection by giving her new joy through her granddaughter and great-granddaughter. God restored her passion for helping women find Jesus and discover their purpose. Now she lives in anticipation of the future He has planned for her. He has filled her life with good things.

The Lord fills our lives in many ways, some of which I have listed below. As you read the related Scripture, may you receive joy and encouragement for your journey. Perhaps you can add other truths as well.

- He fills us with joy in His presence (Psalm 16:11).
- He fills us with power through the Holy Spirit (Romans 15:13).
- He fills us with wisdom (James 1:5).
- He fills our longings and our deepest desires (Psalm 37:4).
- He fills our lives with good things (Psalm 103:5).
- He fills us with strength when we are weak (2 Corinthians 12:9).
- He fills us with anticipation of the future (Isaiah 43:18–19).
- He fills us with courage to take risks (Deuteronomy 31:6).
- He fills us with awe when we look at His creation (Psalm 103:22).
- He fills us with love for Him and others (Ephesians 5:2).
- He fills us with light in the darkness (John 8:12).

In the face of loss, disappointment, or hopelessness, He will fill up our empty spaces. He may give us a glimpse of a purpose we've never considered. And as we step into that new purpose, God will walk beside us and show us which steps to take.

During our lives, we will walk into happy, joyous experiences that brighten our day. We may also be bombarded with sad, shocking events that can change our lives in a moment. Whatever we experience, we must never lose hope. God is our source of hope, joy, peace, and power.

My Personal Prayer:

_____

_____

_____

_____

_____

_____

_____

_____

_____

_____

Bible Memory Verse:

You have shown me the way of life, and you will fill me with
the joy of your presence. (Acts 2:28)

Chapter Challenge:

• Think of a time when heartache threatened to overcome you, but God filled you with peace and assurance that He would protect you and keep you strong. Journal about it here.

_____

_____

_____

_____

_____

_____

_____

_____

• Remember Gretchen's prayer to God for forgiveness, even though it had been fifteen years since her wrong decision had kept her from seeing her son Ronald one more time. God forgave her, whispered words of assurance, and brought relief. Do you need to ask God's forgiveness for something, even something that may have happened a long time ago? He will hear and answer your prayer. He is a loving and accepting Father.

_____

_____

_____

_____

_____

_____

_____

_____

- In what ways has God filled your empty spaces? Has he resolved a separation within your family? Brought you a new friend? Given you a wonderful, godly spouse? Helped you begin a new career? Taken you on a great adventure? Tell a friend what God has done for you.

Chapter 5

From Brokenness to Beauty
Sara Strong

"Where is my baby sister?"

Sara dashed around the room, looking for her sister, Margie. After questioning every volunteer assigned to the nursery that Sunday morning, one calmly told her, "A man and lady picked her up."

As I listened to this bit of drama during a phone call from my friend Sara last week, I wondered what else she would reveal to me this morning at Panera.

When I walked into the restaurant that day, Sara's joy-filled countenance distinguished her from every other woman in the room. A lovely woman in her fifties, she stood out from the preteen girls, the frowning women with stress etched on their faces, the lonely ones, and the loud attention-getters.

I wandered to the back table where she sat.

"Hi, Gail. Ready for some breakfast?"

While Sara chose a blueberry muffin, fruit, and coffee at the counter, I requested my favorite spinach quiche and a caramel latte. After settling back at our table, we each took our first delicious bite and drank a few sips of our coffee.

That was when Sara began the story of her two-and-a-half-year-old sister who disappeared from church that long-ago Sunday morning. "In my five-year-old mind, I thought I'd see my baby sister at home. When my six-year-old brother, Ramon, and I bounded off the Sunday school bus, I ran inside and asked my mom and dad, 'Where's Margie?' They only looked at me, not answering my question."

"Did your family ever find out who took her or what happened to her?" I said.

"Many years later, when I was in my forties, I discovered that the state took her that day. Before we leave this morning, Gail, I'll tell you the whole story."

The story might be sad, but at least Sara had eventually found her sister.

Sara continued, "My world changed that day. I had always taken care of my little sister as though she were my own baby. I fed her, dressed her, and held her when she cried. The void her absence left in my heart was indescribable. I carried that sorrow and emptiness in my heart every day."

Another Sorrow

"Two weeks after my sister was taken, and shortly before my sixth birthday, my mom died unexpectedly from a blood infection that spread quickly through her body. I thought my mom hung the moon and stars. But what five-year-old girl doesn't? In reality, my mom was a broken woman, addicted to alcohol. She was unable to be a real mother to us.

"The year before, she and my dad stayed out partying one night. Because he was drunk, he crashed the car. She was thrown out and landed in a cornfield. My dad did the unimaginable—he left the scene."

I hesitated, taking a moment to digest what this man had done. "I can't fathom your dad leaving your mom in that field."

"I have no idea what his thoughts may have been in that moment.

All I know is he never could connect emotionally with our family or with life."

"How long did she lie there alone? Did someone find her?"

"We don't know how long she suffered in that field alone. But an old man, walking his dog in the middle of the night, heard her faraway cries and called for help. Mom had broken her back and sustained many internal injuries. She became paralyzed from the waist down. A year later, she died."

I had experienced life without emotional connection from my parents, but Sara's need for love and care ran much deeper.

Sara said, "The day of her death was traumatic for all of us, and the drama continued after her passing. It was a Saturday afternoon, and Ramon and I had gone outside to play with the neighbor children. Soon our aunts and uncles began to arrive with their children, and they all gathered in our yard. They wouldn't let us go inside. No one explained anything to us, but I knew something was happening."

"It seems as if your trauma would have heightened at that point, Sara."

"It was agony to stand there, knowing nothing. Soon my dad came out of the house and walked over to the swing set, where Ramon and I sat motionless on the plastic seats. Dad didn't kneel down or pull us into his arms. He merely stood in front of us and said, 'I'm sorry to tell you that your mom has died.'"

Sara explained that she dashed past her dad and ran into the house as fast as she could. One of the nurses her family had personally hired to care for her mother stood in the hallway, but she brushed past her and raced into her mother's room. She shook her mom, begging her to open her eyes. The nurse rushed inside the bedroom and gently pulled Sara away from the bed.

"The nurse led me outside to the grass, a little distance from the crowd that had gathered," Sara said, a few tears dropping from her red-rimmed eyes. "The EMTs wheeled a cart inside the house. They returned with my mother, who was covered with a white sheet, and lifted the cart into the ambulance."

I couldn't imagine what her young heart must have felt in that moment.

"When the ambulance pulled away," she said, "I ran after it, screaming, 'Bring back my mommy.'

"The ambulance stopped. One of the EMTs climbed out, came over to me, and crouched down beside me. 'Child, stop running. You'll hurt yourself.' Then he motioned for someone in the crowd to come and get me."

Tears ran from my eyes as I pictured Sara's trauma and heartache. "Sara, I'm sorry you lost your mother in such a painful way, at such a young age. Did you have someone to support you?"

"Only a few people in our church. My father was unable to comfort Ramon and me. He was an alcoholic and didn't show affection. Even when Mom was alive, he was an absentee father, either on a binge or serving short stints in jail. He came home every couple of weeks, stayed a few days, and left again.

"I longed for a dad and was excited every time he came home. I always threw my arms around him, but he barely responded. The only good times were when he brought food home, and we ate together.

"My dad took Ramon and me to my mother's funeral, which took place five days later, on her thirty-second birthday. That scene was about as dramatic as the day she died. This was also the day my dad kissed Ramon and me on the cheek and said goodbye. We never saw him again. We stood in the driveway, orphans without a mother or father."

I gasped. "No, Sara. Who took care of you?"

Alone and Displaced

"That day, one of our adult cousins came and took us home with them. We stayed there for three months, while my family tried to decide what to do with us.

"During that time, my cousins abused my brother and me emotionally. I started wetting the bed, and they chose to humiliate me by forcing me to wear a diaper at night. This continued throughout the time we were there. Only later did I learn bed-wetting was a result of my trauma.

"My brother and I were given the dirty jobs, like cleaning out their pigpen. Our cousins had two daughters about our age, and we were literally treated like unwanted, mistreated stepchildren."

I wanted to scream. How could those cousins have been so cruel?

"We became a burden to them and were left uncared for. If I talked about my mom, they disciplined me. Very quickly, I learned not to cry or talk about her around them. Instead, I cried into my pillow at night, feeling lonely without my mom. But I made sure no one heard me, for fear of what they would do."

The blatant emotional abuse to these two innocent young children left them scarred forever.

Without a Home

"None of my large family wanted us or could care for us, so we became wards of the state. Ramon and I were placed together in a foster home. I was six years old and Ramon was seven."

My heart sank. "I'm sorry for the despair you must have felt."

"Our new foster home turned out to be a house of horrors and perversion. During our first week there, my foster father began sexually abusing me. I was only six. The abuse continued nearly every day for almost ten months. I had no safe place. That man stole any semblance of innocence that remained in me.

"I told my teacher what was happening at home. She said, 'Stop spreading lies.'

"I concluded that every first grader lived like this. I decided to put up with whatever happened, because no one was going to help my brother and me."

"Sara, I'm grateful that you feel free to share these shocking stories with me. I believe Jesus will use your story to show compassion and give hope to others who have suffered severely, as you have."

"Thank you, Gail. It helps to confide in you. I believe God brought us together so we could become friends and support each other emotionally. I think we will be forever friends."

"I agree, Sara. We will also relish this special friendship handcrafted by God."

False Hope

"Finally, after ten months of abuse in this foster home, a couple who couldn't have their own children expressed interest in adopting us. I later learned the couple chose us from a catalog of hard-to-adopt children. That became our label within the state, primarily because of our age but also because they wanted to keep us siblings together if possible. I was seven and Ramon was eight years old."

I let out a sigh as I pushed away my unfinished quiche, having lost my appetite. But at least she and Ramon found another family. "Finally, you were free."

"We thought so, but it didn't last."

With glazed eyes, Sara turned and looked across the restaurant. I waited, uncertain what she would tell me next, but it sounded as if something had dashed her hopes of living with loving, understanding parents.

Sara looked back at me and took a sip of her coffee before telling me more. "Our new parents picked us up, and on the ride to our forever home, the mom—Beverly—said, 'You can call us Gordon and Beverly until you're ready to call us Mom and Dad.'

"Within a few days, Ramon and I started saying Dad instead of Gordon, probably because we never had a father who was consistently in our lives, although we wanted one. We continued to call our new mom Beverly.

"Whenever we talked about our mom who died, we referred to her as our 'real mom.' I didn't know any other way to describe her. Words like 'biological' were not part of my vocabulary at age seven. We weren't yet ready to call Beverly our mom."

Tears formed in Sara's eyes, surely with renewed heartache from missing her real mother.

"It's understandable that you couldn't call her your mom."

Sara explained, "Our new dad was wonderful and seemed delighted to have the two of us. On the other hand, my adoptive mother became obsessed with turning my brother and me into polite, well-mannered, well-behaved children. But she didn't realize that, in our childhood home, Ramon and I had never eaten at a table or had a family meal. We had no routine and very little adult supervision. We were used to taking care of ourselves.

"Even though Beverly gave us permission to call her Mom, I always referred to my birth mom as my 'real mom.' And Beverly didn't allow the transition to happen naturally.

"The day that Beverly forced me to start calling her 'Mom' was one of the worst days of my life."

The horrified look on Sara's face told me she was reliving that day.

She said, "Beverly yelled at me, 'From this day on, you will call me Mom. You call Gordon your dad, so you will call me Mom. I am your real mom. Your biological mom is dead.'"

I hung my head, trying to absorb the reality of what had happened to my friend. "How cruel. What did you do when she said that?"

"I turned and ran upstairs, then I lunged onto my bed, sobbing and shouting, 'You are not my mom. I want my real mom back!'"

I reached across the table and squeezed Sara's hand. "You were still so young and had no one to love you. My heart breaks for you, Sara. No child should ever be deprived of love."

Sara said, "Anger shot out of my heart. I was devastated that Beverly would try to replace my mom. What made it even harder was that, from the day my mom died, no one had given me time or space to grieve her. In my mind, this current incident killed the possibility of ever grieving.

"In that moment, I made a decision: I would always act as if I were okay and would never let anyone see me cry. I carried that childhood determination into my early forties. No matter where I turned, I found no love or acceptance.

"Beverly's blatant rejection of me was even more horrifying than having to call her Mom. She took out her disappointment in me as her chosen daughter by physically, emotionally, and verbally abusing me."

My heart paused. I thought Sara had already reached the height of rejection, and now this.

Sara and I both cried, reaching for our napkins to wipe our tears. We needed no words.

Finally, I said, "Sara, I can't imagine this depth of depravity."

"During my first four years with my adoptive parents, my adoptive dad was unaware of the abuse taking place when he wasn't home."

A child in the next booth began crying, which heightened the drama.

"On several occasions, my dad pulled Beverly away from me when she spanked me multiple times. When he wasn't around, she spanked me with a metal spatula.

"On the fifth and final year, the abuse intensified. Then came a breakthrough. My dad saw how terrified Ramon and I were of her, and he also noticed our bruises. That was when he took the two of us to a doctor. This began the process of documenting the abuse so he could legally take custody of us, remove us from the home, and leave."

A New Start

Finally, a way of escape. "Did your father succeed in keeping you safe, Sara?"

"Because of the five years of abuse by my adoptive mother and the doctor's documentation, proving the physical abuse, the judge awarded custody of us to my adoptive dad. Freedom finally came when my parents divorced and my dad moved to Florida with Ramon and me to start afresh."

I asked, "What kind of relationship did you and Ramon have with your dad in Florida?"

"He was a good dad. However, he didn't know how to respond to Ramon's angry words and disengagement.

"Also, he was unaware of all the abuse I'd been through with my cousins for three months and the foster parents for ten months. He knew I carried baggage related to my adoptive mother's abuse, but he didn't know how to help me deal with it.

"My dad did the best he could, but he and I went through many challenges during my teen years. He was a perfectionist; I was a broken, wounded girl. I moved out the month I turned eighteen, because I felt I could never meet his expectations."

Sara's dad seemed like a kind person, but I could understand how her trauma was too deep for him to handle.

The Search Begins

"Before I left my dad's home, he sat me down and said, 'Sara, now that you're eighteen, I can show you this letter I received a few years ago. It's about a Social Security refund due to you three children.'

"I stared at the names in the letter: Sara, Ramon—and Mary Ann. My heart pounded as I realized someone must have given my sister the name Mary Ann. After all these years, I couldn't believe I was looking at a name that might help me find my long-lost sister."

My heart pounded too. "Finally, Sara. A lead you could follow."

"From the time I was eighteen years old, I searched for my sister off and on. In those days, we had no internet. However, Oprah Winfrey's show included a segment called, 'Where Are They Now?' I called the toll-free number on the screen. The search cost $90, which took a lot out of my low monthly pay, but I was desperate.

"Unfortunately, my sister's adoptive parents had given her their last name: Miller, a common name. After two years of sending progress reports to me, the company discontinued the search."

This seemed like a dead end to me.

Sara continued, "After searching for my sister for more than thirty years, I finally gave up and surrendered her to the Lord. I prayed, 'If we're never reunited on earth, please let her come to know You, so we can reunite in heaven.'"

I was moved by the emotional depth of Sara's prayer and the obvious spiritual growth that allowed her to let go of her sister and entrust her to the Lord.

"Sara, what a beautiful, moving prayer. Your search clearly helped you grow closer to God. I envision you reaching out your arms during your prayer as if laying your precious sister in His arms."

"Yes, Gail, it was an amazing moment in my life because I felt close to God. I knew He would find my sister and help her find Jesus."

I silently praised God for her continuing belief in God's goodness.

Family Line

I asked, "Did you ever sense God wanting you to pursue another avenue?"

"Amazingly, in 2019, a friend gave me an Ancestry DNA kit. I didn't have to wait long for an answer. I immediately matched with two young adults, both of them a very close match. I reached out to someone named Nancy.

"Six months later, I received a text from Nancy that stated, 'I think you may be my aunt.'"

I said, "That's amazing. What a clear answer to your prayer of faith. How did you feel?"

"My excitement grew. Nancy and I talked by phone a few days later. She told me her mom's name was Mary Ann. Then Nancy added, 'My mom—your sister—was raised by a pastor and his wife.'"

"You must have been eager to meet that couple."

"Definitely. And when my niece, Nancy, introduced me to the pastor and his wife, Gloria, in 2020, the full story began to take shape. Gloria confirmed that the state removed my sister from the church when she was two and a half and brought her to Gloria's home, only an hour from my home at that time.

"Gloria also said that wasn't the first time the state had removed my sister from our home. It began when she was only nine months old. Whenever our mother was in the hospital, the state brought my sister to Gloria and her husband to foster until our mom could care for her again."

I was moved by the willingness of this couple to provide love and care for Margie. "Sara, I wonder why the state didn't help you and your brother."

"I realized that Ramon and I were never reported to the state as neglected children, as my baby sister, Margie, had been. When our mom was hospitalized on and off after the accident, Ramon and I were cared for by various adults who would come in and out to check on Dad and us. Sometimes they took us to their own homes. Margie was in the state system; we were not.

"When our mom died, the state automatically contacted Gloria to let her know. The social worker asked if they wanted to adopt my sister, and they didn't hesitate. However, since the state was unaware of our need, the social worker didn't also offer Ramon and me for adoption.

"While Gloria and I were together, she told me something that filled up my longing heart. 'Often when the state brought Mary Ann to us to foster for a while, they mentioned "the older sister who takes care of Mary Ann." I've been praying for you for years, Sara. Now that I've met you, I think of you as my other daughter from the same mother.'"

Sara felt neglected and unloved, yet God had never forgotten her.

"I was stunned by Gloria's words. Through my tears, I thanked this dear woman and silently thanked God for providing prayers for me all the years I pined for my baby sister and searched for her.

"The sad part is that, even though God obviously chose this wonderful pastor and his wife to raise my sister from an early age, Mary Ann ended up looking for love in all the wrong places. According to Gloria, my sister was born with fetal alcohol syndrome and is now addicted to alcohol. Her many bad choices led her down a broken path."

Such a disappointment to Sara after never giving up on the dream of finding her sister and building a special bond with her.

Accepting the Truth

I wondered how the reality of Mary Ann's life had affected Sara.

She said, "I was shocked to learn that my sister's life paralleled our mother's. Now I understood the cause of Mary Ann's erratic behavior that Gloria had described, but it took me six weeks to call her.

"Disappointment overwhelmed me. My reunion with my sister would no longer be the happy event I'd dreamed of my entire life. I had pictured fun sisterly talks, shopping trips, and belly laughs. I'd wanted a confidant, but that would never happen.

"During those six weeks, I thought about the love and acceptance Gloria and her husband had poured into Mary Ann's life. Yet, Mary Ann was never able to absorb their kind words and actions because of the fetal alcohol syndrome.

"My heart gravitated to helping women, especially those in jail, who felt unloved. Perhaps they weren't able to absorb love and acceptance for the same reason Mary Ann couldn't. Or maybe they had no one who truly loved and cared about them while they were growing up.

"I heard of a weekly jail ministry, and I joined the group. I longed to pour hope into the women's hearts. To show them genuine love and interest. To share words from the Bible that would bring them closer to knowing Jesus.

"The days I spent encouraging incarcerated women brought me the joy and fulfillment I had missed in my life. I knew this was God's path for me."

My admiration for Sara grew deeper. "I'm glad you discovered that fulfilling ministry."

"This ministry was perfect for me. But I still hadn't called my sister, and God had something to say about that. One Sunday morning in 2021, I woke up around four thirty with my sister on my mind.

"I talked with the Lord, cried, worshiped Him, and prayed and cried some more. That was when the Holy Spirit spoke clearly to me: *You minister to women in the jail and have a heart for some of the most broken of women. You have pined for your sister your entire life. Now I've brought her back to you, but her life is too messy for you to get involved.*

"A godly sorrow and different kind of grief swept over me. I spent several hours confessing and repenting of my sin. Until that morning with God, ninety-five percent of my brokenness and pain was a result of someone else's actions: abuse, rejection, abandonment. Now I came face-to-face with my own wickedness of self-righteousness, selfishness, pride, and judgment.

"I thought I knew how to love, but I didn't. It was as though God said, I will show you how to love. He used my sister to show me how to love as He loves. Loving while expecting nothing in return. Loving when I'm not loved back. Loving even if I see no change. God exposed the sinfulness of my heart to prepare me to show unconditional love to my sister."

The First Connection

I envisioned a connection coming.

"Because of my unforgettable time with God, I was eager to call my sister. At the age of fifty, I'd finally get to hear her voice. She was now forty-seven.

"After a few rings, Mary Ann answered. Her daughter had paved the way by telling her that she and I had talked. Mary Ann seemed grateful to talk to me. I listened to her countless questions about our parents, and she talked about the loving mom and dad who'd raised her. She also asked about Ramon. He had made many unfortunate life choices, and we were no longer in touch, but I told her a simple story I remembered about Ramon from our earlier years. Mary Ann had no memory of her early life and knew only what her adoptive parents had told her.

"On the verge of tears, I told Mary Ann, 'You were my baby. I loved caring for you and was devastated when they took you away. I've pined for you my entire life.' Her soft response showed that she felt loved and valued by me in that moment. I'm grateful she had loving adoptive parents."

I paused a moment, taking in everything Sara had related to me.

"I can't imagine what it meant to Mary Ann to hear your voice and to know you had looked for her."

Sara responded, "At the end of our hour-long conversation, my sister told me, 'Sara, this has been the best day of my life.' My heart melted."

I smiled. What a great way to end their first call.

"I treasure her words. We're both grateful that we reconnected, and we're maintaining our new relationship. But because of the trauma in her life and mine, I sense we were both hesitant to reveal everything we had been through. However, I believe God is at work in both our lives, and I'll continue praying for Mary Ann."

Continuing Turmoil

Then I remembered her brother. "Did you ever contact Ramon to tell him you'd found your sister?"

"Yes, but that became a hurtful journey for me. When we were growing up, Ramon and I were close. We had some difficult times while we lived at our dad's house, but we were teenagers. After Ramon left home at age eighteen, he seemed to lose mental control and began making dangerous decisions. He's been in and out of prison his whole life, until the last seven years.

"A year and a half ago, Ramon reconnected with our dad and me. The two of them talk by phone frequently. Unfortunately, when Ramon learned I had found our baby sister in 2021, he became enraged. He publicly threatened my children and me on social media. We all had to block him from our accounts and phones.

"After hearing about my sister's lifelong struggles and observing my brother's destructive behavior, I'm convinced he was born with fetal alcohol syndrome, as she was. They both have trouble connecting with life and making wise decisions. I will never know how I escaped being born with fetal alcohol syndrome."

A double heartache for Sara. She understood the reason for her brother and sister's behavior, but she still had to watch the results of their destructive choices.

"In the midst of this turmoil, God worked in my heart. Gently, He showed me I needed to forgive Ramon. I forgave him in October 2021. Repenting of my thoughts about him and forgiving his behavior helped me distance myself from Ramon. Whenever my fear of him rises, I remind myself that God is my shield and protector."

An Unexpected Introduction

Sensing that both of us needed a break, I said to Sara, "How about another cup of coffee?"

"Good idea. Many things happened in my past, and I have more to tell you."

It felt good to stand and take in the scene around me. I heard the sound of little ones, both giggles and cries. Studious young people sat in the back corner, furiously typing on their computers. Two women laughed together, obviously enjoying each other's company.

After receiving our fresh cups of coffee at the counter, we sauntered back to our table while bringing up a few lighthearted incidents to laugh about. I smiled at Sara as I slid into our booth. "I'm curious about your later life."

"Some church friends set me up on a blind date with a fellow they knew. Hank and I dated for a few months and got married in March 1992. While we were dating, we enjoyed mutual interests and perspectives, but like many couples, we laid aside personality differences that didn't seem to matter at the time.

"Church was the focal point of the week for us. We both volunteered where needed. Soon our first son, Cole, came along, followed by Walker and Olivia."

A Downhill Course

"My husband and I had a wonderful life together until the final three years of our marriage. With no explanation, Hank began undermining my authority with the children. He ordered me to stop disciplining Walker, who was seventeen. I remained a positive influence over Cole, who was nineteen, and Olivia, sixteen.

"I quickly saw the effects of Hank's decision to give Walker free rein of his life. Walker began making unwise choices about the friends he spent time with, and his grades were suffering.

"Hank owned a telecommunications business that installed huge phone systems in buildings. Suddenly, he sold his business and took a job driving a bus for Disney. With his drastic pay cut, our financial stability began falling apart. I never heard Hank make any business calls or say anything that indicated he was making an effort to find a job with higher pay. I would learn later that he purposely took a job well below his ability in order to avoid having to contribute financially to our family."

I tried to temper my disappointment. "Things changed behind the scenes."

"Yes. We could no longer make mortgage payments, so we were forced into a short sale on the house we'd lived in for more than twenty years. I discovered Hank hadn't made any financial provision for our future or for a place for us to live after the house sold. He always took care of things like this, so I wasn't prepared to face the dilemma ahead of us."

Their family foundation had crumbled. I wondered where this was going.

"The only solution I saw at that time was for him and Walker to move in with his parents and for Cole, Olivia, and me to live with my father. Hank agreed. I viewed this as a temporary arrangement until we could build up our resources. Even though our marriage was strained, divorce was never on my mind.

"In June, before the three of us moved to my dad's, I told Walker, 'I want you to come with us. But if I can't parent you, you can't come.'

"Walker looked me straight in the eye, defiance on his face, and said, 'I don't need parenting.'"

A Refuge

With all the turmoil swirling around Sara, I was glad she had a place to go.

"My dad welcomed the three of us into his home, giving us a roof over our heads and a safe place to live. At age nineteen, Cole worked for a Christian ministry and earned an income. I had responsibility for sixteen-year-old Olivia. My job paid the bills and covered Olivia's expenses. Dad helped with groceries.

"Being in Dad's home gave me the needed privacy to process all that had happened. I laid my early years of trauma alongside Hank's unexpected disengagement in our marriage and saw only rejection. My dad couldn't lift me up spiritually or help with my healing, but his presence in my life brought comfort."

At least they provided consistent companionship for each other.

Truth Revealed

I asked, "What happened next with the children?"

"Walker lived with his dad from June to December. During that time, Olivia wanted the same freedom Walker had, so she turned on me and moved in with her dad.

"In December, after five weeks with her father, Olivia called me, sobbing. 'Mom, can you come get me at school?'

"When I arrived, Olivia sat on a bench outside the school. She shivered in her shorts and sleeveless top. Walker was supposed to pick her up, but he never showed."

With her nurturing heart, Sara must have struggled with seeing her daughter uncared for.

"My heart broke to see Olivia that way, but at least she wanted to come home with me. As soon as we arrived, she went into my bedroom and threw herself on the bed. 'Mom, you're going to be so upset. Dad moved in with his girlfriend. He has nothing to do with us.'

"I'd thought Hank was taking care of Walker and Olivia at his parents' home. I had no idea of his affair. Now I realized I no longer knew this man. He was not the man I fell in love with and married."

I said, "What about Walker? Did he still live at his grandparents' home?"

"About the time I heard about Hank's infidelity, Walker showed up on my doorstep, sobbing like a baby. I hugged him and welcomed him inside. His father had kicked him out, and Walker wanted me to 'parent' him again. After spending time helping him deal with the pain of his father's rejection, we began to rebuild our relationship."

Wanting to encourage Sara, I laid my hand on hers. "Although it was traumatic to watch Walker and Olivia choose to live with Hank, they obviously knew they could return to you because you were always there for them."

"The result was bittersweet. I was grateful the four of us could be together again, but the nightmare continued."

Continuing Nightmare

I braced myself for the next episode.

"On January 2, Hank served me with divorce papers. By then, unknown to me, the only assets we had were two storage units filled with our furniture and $1,600 in our joint bank account. This meant Hank had almost depleted our account along with everything else we had accumulated. The full picture finally became clear. Hank had purposely given up his stable business and become underemployed to prepare to file for divorce.

"We went to court. The judge sided with Hank. Because he worked for the minimum wage by then, the judge required him to give me only sixty-five dollars per week in child support for Olivia. He did not require Hank to pay any medical bills. The judge also decided to emancipate our middle son, Walker, which meant Hank was released from providing financial support for him."

"Sara, how shocking. I can't believe the judge's actions."

"The final blow came when the judge looked at me and said, 'You are eligible to receive alimony, but Hank is unable to pay. Therefore, I am awarding you one dollar for now to keep the door open, should Hank ever become able to pay alimony.'

"I was stunned. In my wildest imagination, I never dreamed my marriage would end this way. A year and a half ago, I went back to court to sue for alimony. But Hank countersued, and I couldn't afford an attorney. The Lord showed me I needed to cancel my lawsuit.

"Hank didn't want anything out of our twenty-one years of marriage. Worse, he turned his back on his children. He soon married the woman he'd had the affair with."

I asked who came alongside to support her. A sad answer came.

"I thought my church would rally around me, especially under the circumstances. Instead, they ostracized me, after I'd worshiped in and served that church for thirty years. I was without a church family. The pain deepened when some of my closest church friends pulled out of our friendships. I felt abandoned by people who loved God but evidently didn't care about me. My church's response to my devastating situation remains a mystery."

Journey of Healing

"In the past," she said, "the stress would have immobilized me. However, this time my usual stress didn't surface. My marriage had dissolved and all my dreams had vanished, but God took care of me. I continually express my thanks to God for giving me a full-time job with a higher salary. And I lived in my dad's home for almost three years until I could afford to rent a condo. By then, the children were on their own."

"Sara, tell me more about how God helped you stay strong in spite of your great losses."

"God used my crisis to expand my faith and enlarge my trust in Him. He filled me with new love for His Word. Being in the Word lifted my focus to Jesus and kept me from dwelling on my circumstances. God's Word stabilized me as I began to heal from my trauma.

"I heard about an international Christian ministry that helps women heal from their pain and trauma through transformational discipleship. I joined their five-year program, and experienced deep healing and transformation in my life."

I learned from Sara that this ministry helps turn head knowledge of Scripture into heart knowledge, which transforms them more and more into the image of Jesus and sets them free to become who God created them to be.

"Three years before I finished this program, the leaders began training and equipping me to serve with them while continuing my own healing. I'm still working with this ministry, along with my career in marketing and design. The sweetest part of my life, though, is watching women experience freedom, many of them for the first time."

I pondered Sara's amazing healing and transformation, and the opportunity she's had to become part of this healing ministry that fills her with joy. "Sara, your smile, your love for people, and your gentle spirit obviously make a difference in the way these wounded women view themselves."

New Horizons

"I'm still in awe of all God has done for me. After I'd rented my condo for five years, the owners sold the building, so I moved back in with my dad. He is a wonderful papa, and my three grown children's best friend. Cole asked him to be best man in his wedding."

"That brings tears to my eyes, Sara. After all your children have been through, it is so sweet that they feel close to your dad and let him love them. Tell me more about your children."

"Cole and his wife, Skye, live in California. They hope to start their family in the next several years.

"My daughter, Oliva, has gone through some turbulent times. Three years ago, she became pregnant, and I invited her to move in with Dad and me so I could help her in her new life as a single mom. Her adorable two-year-old, curly-haired daughter, Dakota, brings us all a lot of joy.

"Walker is married to Angela and they have two girls, ages seven and five. Because they live in Maryland, we FaceTime often. We all look forward to being together during my annual fall trips.

"Nothing fills my heart more than having time and freedom to pour love into the lives of my children and grandchildren by celebrating who they are, laughing with them, and joining their activities whenever we're together.

"My initial time at Dad's place proved to be God's path of redemption. God rescued me from being consumed by my trauma. When I returned to Dad's home, I experienced additional redemption through the closeness with my children and grandchildren."

"Sara, it's sweet to picture the peace and calm in your life now. I'm happy for you and grateful to God."

"I'll never completely forget the abuse, neglect, and rejection of my past. Yet God brought beauty out of ashes as described in this beautiful Bible verse:

> To all who mourn in Israel, he will give a crown of beauty for ashes, a joyous blessing instead of mourning, festive praise instead of despair. In their righteousness, they will be like great oaks that the LORD has planted for his own glory. (Isaiah 61:3)

"Through my brokenness, I am able to show others the unconditional love and acceptance of God."

As Sara gradually shared her unbelievable life with me that day in Panera, I could hardly absorb all she had survived. The enemy used evil people to keep Sara captive to fear. When her life collapsed, she thought all hope of a joyful and fulfilling life had died. Sara's bondage seemed impossible to break.

However, our powerful God rescued Sara out of the abyss. He brought inner healing and gave Sara freedom to minister to needy women out of her own traumatic experiences.

Sara's transformation prepared her to lead a life of beauty and equipped her to walk into God's unfolding plans for her.

You also may have had a traumatic, devastating, shameful past you can't seem to let go of. God knows where you've been and what you've experienced, so you have nothing to hide, nothing to be ashamed of. You can talk to the Lord honestly and freely.

God wants you to trust Him to deliver you from reminders of your past so you can look forward to your future with joy. He wants you to take His hand and follow Him out of hiding so you can receive healing.

Ask God to lead you to a counselor or organization that can help you find inner healing as Sara did. Read God's Word, where you will find Jesus healing people. Psalm 147:3 says, "He heals the brokenhearted and bandages their wounds."

Regardless of the devastating experiences of your past or your struggles in the present, God wants you to know He has a plan for your future.

> For I know the plans I have for you," says the LORD. "They are plans for good and not for disaster, to give you a future and a hope." (Jeremiah 29:11)

God waits to rescue, love, and take care of you. He wants to transform your life so you can become more like Him. He will help you renew your mind so you can focus on Him and the truth of His words.

God wants you to experience beauty for brokenness and give you courage to walk into a new future with Him.

My Personal Prayer:

_____

_____

_____

_____

_____

_____

_____

_____

_____

Bible Memory Verse:

Don't copy the behavior and customs of this world, but let God transform you into a new person by changing the way you think. Then you will learn to know God's will for you, which is good and pleasing and perfect. (Romans 12:2)

Chapter Challenge:

- Does a past experience hinder you from moving forward in life? Acknowledge this to God and let Him take away the power of that experience. Ask Him to give you courage and wisdom to step forward. Don't hesitate to visit a Christian counselor or talk to a trusted friend who can give you the help you need.

- Quiet your heart before the Lord and invite the Holy Spirit to shine His light and truth into every hidden area of your heart. Write down what He reveals to you. Pray about it, asking His forgiveness if needed, and releasing it to Him.

_____

_____

_____

_____

_____

_____

- Do you face an impossible situation with a family member and don't see a solution? Ask forgiveness for any part you may have had in the situation. Ask God to give you a word to say or action to take that will bring a solution. Remember, nothing is impossible with God.

_____

_____

_____

_____

_____

_____

Chapter 6

From Outer Pain to Inner Peace
Julie Ann Payne

"*A* person with blond hair and blue eyes does not look Italian, right?"

I laughed at Julie's inquiry. Since she's 100 percent Italian, she would know. I couldn't help wondering why she asked.

As we lingered after our monthly writers' meeting, she explained her perplexing question. "My dad had blond hair and blue eyes, and no one ever guessed his nationality. So, due to anti-Italian prejudice, and before he joined the navy to serve in the Korean War, he chose to change his last name from Piantedosi to Payne. He felt a European flair would be more appropriate for his fair features. But this surname would come to haunt me in elementary school and for years to come."

"I can tell there's a fascinating story behind this, Julie. Let's get together for lunch, and you can tell me more."

"I know of a great Italian restaurant," she said.

"I already know I'll order lasagna."

Before I knew it, our planned lunch was upon us. After settling at our table that day, surrounded by colorful decor and boisterous laughter, I smiled at Julie. "We've been friends for a long time, but I think I'm going to learn some new things about you."

"You're right. A lot of it is sad and truly hurt me," Julie said, "but some special things happened as well."

I studied the menu. "Let's order, then we can talk while we wait for our food."

Several minutes later, Julie began. "I struggled to discover why my dad chose to change his last name to Payne. After talking to my mom, the only conclusion I could draw was that he named himself after the famed jazz musician Cecil Payne. Both Cecil and my dad played the saxophone, and both were born in Brooklyn, New York, only nine years apart."

"It sounds as if your father loved music."

"Yes, and I could imagine my dad having a special affinity toward Cecil, since they both played the saxophone. Maybe my dad looked up to him. I never found out the real reason, because he passed away when I was only fourteen."

Seeing tears in her eyes, I laid my hand on hers. "I'm sorry to hear that, Julie. Please tell me more about your family."

"My mom and dad married in May 1953. Since Mom was a few years older than my dad, she was ready to start a family. I'm the third of five siblings. My parents had their share of trials with us. My oldest brother needed a tracheotomy at birth. Mom miscarried her fifth pregnancy, and I was born two months premature. I was so small that Mom called me Baby Thumbelina. They named me Julie Ann Payne; Julie after my mom and Ann after Saint Anne."

Classroom Insults

Due to her dad's job transfer, Julie's family moved from western New York to Southern California, where she started second grade in a new school. She easily fit in with her classmates, made good grades, and became the teacher's helper.

Julie said, "I was a people pleaser, trying to meet everyone's needs.

Since we lived only a block from school, I quite often invited friends to bring their lunches to my house. On those days, I grabbed something to eat at home and saved my lunch money to buy snacks for my friends when we went to the movies. That made them happy.

"Unfortunately, some kids weren't nice to me. My last name proved to be a real pain, especially with the mean kids at school. The bullies ridiculed me and made me feel rejected and excluded. Outwardly, I smiled and put on the face of a friendly, sweet girl. Inside, I desperately wanted to be liked, but my heart ached because of the few who mocked me and teased me about my name."

"I can't imagine your emotions, Julie, when you became the brunt of your classmates' hurtful words and actions."

She seemed to look straight through me; her eyes glazed over and filled with tears. "It was awful. Their favorite chant was, 'Julie, Julie, what a pain; send her away on a plane.' All my self-doubts rested on those eleven words. They stung and etched themselves deep in my mind.

"Those experiences made me want to please others all the more so I wouldn't be shunned. However, I soon began to believe their words were true."

Absorbed in her story, I barely noticed our server setting our meals on the table and refreshing our drinks. When Julie paused, I said, "This smells delicious."

"I didn't realize I was so hungry," Julie said.

Abandonment

After we exchanged a few more updates, I asked her how she survived all those hurtful words.

Julie whispered, "I'm not sure. I struggled with it for years. Then, when I was thirty, peace came to me in the strangest way."

I leaned forward to catch all the details.

"God hurled a miracle into my life after my live-in boyfriend, Aubrey, broke up with me on Christmas Eve. We had the holidays all planned: festivities with my family that night and airline tickets in hand to spend Christmas Day with his family. But a small quarrel escalated into a full-blown fight. Before I knew it, he took my apartment key and threw my purse, my packed suitcase, and my wrapped gifts out the front door.

"In less than a minute, he jumped into his truck, leaving me standing in the apartment parking lot. Tears filled my eyes, blurring his fading red taillights. All I could feel was the pain of rejection, asking myself, 'What just happened? Who gets dumped on Christmas Eve?'"

Shocked myself, I said, "What a horrible experience. What did you do?"

"After what seemed like hours, I finally drove to my mom's house and crashed on her couch. When I woke up on Christmas Day, the family had gathered. Their first question was, 'Where's Aubrey?'

"Looking down, I told them, 'We're not together anymore.' Fortunately, they didn't press for details. I put on a fake smile and tried to celebrate with my family.

"Later, I confided to my sister the heartbreaking reality that I had nowhere to live. She handed me a key to her home and told me to go there. We'd work out the details later."

An Amazing Encounter

"Thank goodness for family at that scary time of your life."

"That's for sure. I'm grateful for my sister. Exhausted and heartbroken, I fell asleep in her spare bedroom. Then something happened I can describe only as a miracle. I had a one-on-one visit from Jesus, and it changed my life."

My eyes widened. "My goodness, Julie. Did Jesus shine a light to open your eyes?"

"Well, sort of. After tossing and turning in bed, wallowing in my own little pity party, I looked up at what should have been flowered curtains and saw the face of Jesus with a long beard and a crown of thorns. Next to Him was a smaller image of Satan, as we perceive him, with gaunt cheeks and sharp horns. Between the contrasting faces, I saw two white eyes as if God were looking straight at me.

"With my eyes fixed on the scene before me, I whispered, 'How could this be? What is this?'

"Then God spoke to my heart. *Julie, you need to make a decision.* I couldn't believe God would communicate with me this way."

I relished the way the Lord spoke clearly to Julie at such a crucial time.

"I tried to comprehend God Himself reaching all the way down from heaven and finding me. I wasn't even looking for Him. I had given up on God. All those times I begged Him to take away my pain, rejection, and bullying, I felt He never showed up to help me. And now, when I immersed myself in pity, wondering why hurt always seemed to find me, God personally revealed Himself to me and filled me with His presence. That was truly miraculous."

My heart exploded with joy. "Just when you felt lost and lonely, suddenly Jesus was there with you. He said you needed to make a decision?"

"Yes, I had to choose either Jesus's way of righteousness and enjoy spiritual life or Satan's way of sin and suffer spiritual death.

"I knew what I wanted to do. The instant I chose Jesus, a wonderful peace flowed through me from head to toe—a peace I had never felt before.

"God's love filled the void in my heart when I chose Him that Christmas Day. He didn't wait for me to fix my eyes on Him first—He sought me and found me. He didn't want me to be perfect—He accepted me the way He found me, flaws and all. My religion of doing good was transformed into a relationship with the living God. When He reached down from heaven into my sister's guest room that day, He performed a miracle.

"This was all new to me, so I wondered if I'd been born again. Was this what my brother Alfred experienced when he was fourteen?"

Seeing someone else's life change can open a door of understanding.

"Someone had shared the gospel of Jesus Christ with Alfred, and he boldly confessed, 'Praise God! I am saved.' I loved my brother, but I couldn't relate to his newfound obsession with Jesus Christ. I repeatedly taunted him with sarcasm, calling him Alfred the Jesus Freak. His response annoyed me all the more: 'Hallelujah! I'm praying for you, sister.'

"Toting his Bible with him, Alfred tried to convert everyone he knew. I couldn't understand how his life was so radically changed, so I stopped hanging out with him. His new religion impeded our relationship, and we parted ways for a while."

"It's wonderful to see how much godly influence Alfred had in your life, even though you weren't aware of it."

"Yes, and many years later, God worked in my own life. He saved me, changed my heart, and gave me a new perspective. He forgave all my sins and replaced my chaos with His peace.

"God's love became so real and His compassion so tangible, I felt compelled to call my ex-boyfriend, Aubrey, and apologize for my part in our argument on Christmas Eve. We talked for over an hour. That conversation, now bathed in God's love and forgiveness through faith, began to mend our broken relationship and heal our wounded hearts. Our renewed relationship would eventually lead to marriage."

I was amazed by their reconnection. "Julie, I love that you spoke with faith when you talked with Aubrey. Your conversation proved that God had changed your life."

"I'll always remember the miraculous way God helped me begin a relationship with Him." Julie glanced at her watch. "I have more to share, but I guess we should do that on a different day."

I checked the time on my phone. "Text me with a day and time. I look forward to part two."

We hugged before getting into our cars. I sensed a deepening of our friendship that day.

Part Two

About a week later, we settled into a secluded corner at the back of a quieter restaurant, where we could talk undisturbed.

After we handed our menus back to the waitstaff, Julie jumped in where she had left off. "When Aubrey and I started talking about marriage, I suggested we get married that week. I could tell he was startled. Assuming he thought I was pregnant, I quickly said, 'There's no need to wait. We've both been married before, and we're ready.'"

"I didn't know you'd been married before you met Aubrey."

"Yes, unfortunately, it was short lived. That was one reason I was thrilled about our upcoming marriage. When we met with our pastor, he asked a few questions to gauge how prepared we were for marriage, then he agreed to our midweek wedding.

"I couldn't contain my excitement when our wedding day arrived. I worked in my flower shop until one in the afternoon, then flipped over the 'closed' sign. Then I dabbed on some fresh makeup, fluffed my hair, changed into an off-white ruffled dress, reached for my baby's breath bouquet, and headed to the church."

I said, "Undoubtedly, your beauty stunned Aubrey."

"Aubrey met me at the double-door entrance to our small church building, with a big grin on his face. We stood in awe and hugged, knowing we would soon be married. Our pastor joined us in the lobby. He gave us a few instructions and then asked if we were ready. Aubrey and I stated in unison, 'Absolutely.'

"The pastor led Aubrey to the main altar, only ten pews away. As the church pianist played Mendelssohn's 'Wedding March,' I strolled down the short aisle, passing by my sister, her husband, and a couple of friends who came to witness our joyous occasion.

"As Aubrey and I made eye contact, I knew I was ready for our happily ever after in the Lord. One glittering candelabrum on the altar behind us decorated the scene as we pledged our love and devotion to one another before God. No superficial expressions or memorized lines, but honest vows from the heart."

Raising a Family

I was happy for Julie and wondered where they went on their honeymoon.

"We didn't take a honeymoon right away," Julie said. "Instead, we left one month later for a trip to the Florida Panhandle for Aubrey's family reunion. There I met his entire family, which excited me since family is important to me.

"I got pregnant right away. I asked God to let my baby be born later than its due date, since I was still obsessed with what people would think of me. Two weeks past my due date, while teaching my Monday night ladies' Bible study in my home, I patted my bulging belly and chuckled. 'I hope one day to be this pregnant with God's Word.' My friends giggled as a nauseous feeling invaded my body.

"Labor had started. By two o'clock in the morning, we called my mom and sister to meet us at the birthing center, having opted for a midwife. After almost eighteen hours of labor, the cries of a newborn baby filled the room. Joy spread through our hearts as we looked at our precious baby boy, Ryan—God's gift to us."

A new season had begun for Julie and Aubrey.

"When Ryan turned six months old, I became pregnant again. A scheduled trip for a sonogram revealed the thrilling news of another boy. Nine months flew by. Again, in the wee hours of the morning, we called my mom and sister and headed to the birthing center. Once there, the midwife and helpers rushed to prepare. Less than an hour passed, and with one last push, we listened to the wails of our second son.

"But our perplexed midwife shouted over the clamoring cries, 'It's a girl!' We had no pink blanket, no cute dresses, and no princess crib. We hadn't even chosen a girl's name. However, when the midwife handed me our baby, all my anxieties flew away as fast as the winds of a tornado. Aubrey kissed me and we smiled at God's newest gift—our sweet, precious baby daughter. We named her Nicole."

I laughed as I imagined their expressions when they learned the baby was a girl, not a boy. "I'll look forward to seeing their baby pictures sometime."

"We beamed that day, but the reality of parenting two children set in quickly. Aubrey started leaving the house by six in the morning and returning late every night. When he finally came home, he always woke the children, told them he loved them, and went to bed, leaving me with both children wide awake."

"This was certainly an unexpected change, Julie. Did you question Aubrey about his behavior?"

"I told him he needed to be home more and to help out with the children. When I asked why he was coming home late, he gave excuses. A couple of my friends said they had seen him at bars in the evening, but I lacked the courage to confront him on it.

"Finances were another issue. I noticed his income had decreased. Money was also tight at my flower shop. I explained our situation, and told Aubrey he needed to be more responsible in his work and help with his share of the expenses."

"Did that improve your situation?"

"No. My continuing words of frustration flung at him made no difference. I wanted to believe in the possibility that Aubrey suffered from the syndrome that men get when children come into the picture and they aren't ready for a family. Yet, I knew our problem went deeper. Our marriage was drifting."

A Dividing Line

"We had not arranged to dedicate Ryan as a new baby the year before, so Aubrey and I decided to dedicate both Ryan and Nicole to the Lord on Mother's Day. Aubrey had stopped regularly attending church with me, but he promised to meet me that morning.

"The service began, but Aubrey hadn't appeared. Later, I stood at the altar with other couples and their children, my eyes focused on the door. I hoped he would arrive, but he never did. I dedicated our children alone."

My heart hurt for Julie. "Did Aubrey ever explain his actions that day?"

"Not until later. In that moment, rejection descended again. I couldn't understand Aubrey's alienation from me and our little ones.

"God whispered, *Depend on Me; hope in Me; trust only in Me.* I found that hard to do. I chose to find solace in my flower shop during the day while the kids were with a sitter. Pleasing my customers occupied my mind and helped relieve the hurt Aubrey had inflicted on my heart."

I wondered how Aubrey's aloofness and Julie's stressful behavior affected the children.

"On the home front, often our children refused to go to sleep at a decent hour. I couldn't keep them on a schedule. Concerned, I asked my midwife, 'Why are my children so wild and out of sorts? Is that normal?'

"She gave me an answer I didn't want to hear. 'Julie, what you do in moderation, your children will do in excess. Your children reflect you and your home. What's happening at home?'

"Her words made me stop running and take an honest look at my life. I saw a strained marriage, stressed schedules, and rare vacations. I'd even set my time with God on a high, hard-to-reach shelf in my mind. I attended church and Bible studies, walking tall and acting spiritual. But my hectic life had taken its toll on my relationship with God and my family."

I felt the pain of Julie's difficult realization that her life with God and her family was off track.

"When Nicole turned three, Aubrey stated that he'd had enough of me pushing him to work harder, and he was tired of my chaotic lifestyle. He then walked away from our five years of marriage, our two children, and our single-wide mobile home. I was devastated. Depression embittered my mind with thoughts of abandonment, failure, and worthlessness.

"I cried out to God, 'Please help me understand and move forward.' In His love and mercy, God showed me I had become preoccupied with many details and depended on my own ability to squeeze work into every moment. I began to see what Aubrey may have experienced at home.

"After Aubrey left, I felt there was no way for us to reconcile. From time to time, I heard he was back to his old ways of bar hopping. He also did not always keep his promise to spend time with the children.

"One holiday, he had promised to pick up the children for a weekend in Pensacola. Ryan and Nicole sat on the steps with their packed suitcase, waiting for him to come. I called him several times but got no answer. He finally called me to say he was in Pensacola. He had gone without them.'"

Another dashed hope for the children that surely deepened their feeling of rejection.

"After more than a year of rarely speaking to each other, and him either not making an effort to see the children or breaking his promises to them, I filed divorce papers.

"When despair about our breakup tried to overcome me, God gave me grace to accept what had happened. God lifted me out of my sadness, using moments of unexpected humor from my children to remind me that He loved me. The more I focused on Jesus and others, the more He blessed me and provided for my needs."

"What a wonderful Father, who knew exactly how to change your perspective."

A Time of Healing

"I'll never forget the way He took away my sadness and gave me hope. I want to tell you about another experience of hope that happened after my divorce."

I reached for my coffee cup and leaned back against the padded booth. "I'm ready."

"You'll remember how I was ridiculed by some classmates during grade school. I experienced the same kind of humiliation when I gave my testimony in church. The embarrassment revolved around my name again, but this time God brought healing.

"One Sunday, my pastor told the church he was going to ask some members to give a testimony during our regular night of praise. I was excited about sharing how God had changed my life, so I went to his office after the service.

"Pastor, I would like to give my testimony during our praise night. I didn't want to wait to ask you because I'm excited about this opportunity.

"My pastor looked at me with wide eyes of disbelief and sat in silence. Unsure of his thoughts, I presented my request again.

"He seemed puzzled and said, 'You're joking, right?'

"Equally puzzled by his response, I said, 'No, not at all. Please let me tell my story. I didn't want to wait for you to ask others and not give me a chance.'"

I said, "My goodness, this was your pastor. I would think he'd welcome your offer to share your testimony."

"I expected him to. Finally, after what seemed a very long time, he gave a short nod and said, 'Sure.' I exhaled."

Julie's eyes lit up as she continued. "Finally, our night of praise arrived. Even though I was a little nervous, I was eager to share my story.

"The pastor stood at the podium and said, 'Let's begin with someone who asked me if she could speak. Over the years, we've had many testimony nights, but no one has ever asked to give a testimony. However, this member insisted on sharing what God has done in her life.'

"Then, in jest, he said, 'She is a lady who is a Payne in more ways than one.' Amidst laughter, he continued. 'Recently, I found out her middle name is Ann. And that confirmed what I already knew. I introduce to you Julie A. Payne.'

"The crowd laughed again and clapped as I smiled and strode to the front of the stage. As I stood at the podium, I had to look up to heaven, because in that moment, I didn't have the usual knot in my stomach. I didn't feel defeated by the lifelong chant that reverberated in my mind, *Julie, Julie, what a pain; send her away on a plane.* I could have pondered what the congregation thought of me then or become fearful that they'd laugh as soon as I started speaking. None of that happened."

Without thinking, I clapped, too. "That's amazing, Julie. You triumphed!"

"God was definitely with me. That night brought His second miracle for me. He healed my pain and turned my life around a hundred and eighty degrees."

I was eager to hear more from Julie about how God had changed her life.

"Before that night, I often dwelled on the negative things in my life: my dad's death when I was only fourteen, the elementary school bullies, and rejection by the father of my children.

"I diverted my pain by trying to ignore it. I thought that was the right thing to do, but escapism is a dead-end path. Distractions couldn't cure my rejection and heartache. Ignoring my pain simply caused me to suppress my feelings.

"When God took away my pain that night at church, He removed the power of the negative events that ruled my life. When I faced the reality of all that had happened to me, my feelings began to surface. Then I could deal with them in a healthy way. Once in a while, the memory of my past pain stalls me momentarily, but I turn those feelings over to God, and He lifts me up again."

A New Life

I felt proud of Julie. She allowed God to work in her, and He took away her pain. I loved hearing how, when memories come, she turns her feelings over to God.

"When I gave God the ridicule, Aubrey's rejection, and my desire to please others, He showed me how to live on a new path. I allowed His Word to penetrate my heart and mind. I became active in church again and joined a Bible study.

"Whenever I read God's Word, I see His love poured out for me. Instead of focusing on my circumstances, I fix my eyes on Christ, who has given me new strength, steadiness, and security. God's love fills me with joy every day. I allow the Holy Spirit to guide my understanding of God's Word. I let Him lead me each day because I want to align my life with the Lord's good plans for me."

"Julie, you are drinking in the wonders of knowing God and living for Him."

"You know, Gail, I took it hard when Aubrey left and we eventually divorced. But God used that pain to draw me closer to Himself. God also used Aubrey's now-frequent visits with the children to heal me of an attitude of resentment and that monster of rejection. Focused on God, I saw Aubrey's fatherly love and gentle nature more clearly. Through that softening, the Lord enabled us to have an amicable relationship. It was a redemptive act of God, and I'll be forever grateful. Aubrey ended up moving to the Florida Panhandle, yet he remained in touch through phone calls and occasional visits."

"Julie, with all that's happened to you, I'm wondering what your favorite Bible verse is."

"That's easy. Isaiah 65:1 especially touches my heart: 'I was sought by those who did not ask for Me; I was found by those who did not seek Me. I said, "Here I am, here I am," to a nation that was not called by My name.'

"Gail, I was that person. I was not looking for God. But in His love and mercy, He sought me out. He never gave up on me, even though I had given up on Him because of the pain and heartache I'd endured throughout my life.

"Gradually, I recognized that my pain pushed me toward God and prepared me to accept the miracle He had waiting for me on Christmas Day. Now I know, without a doubt, how much He loves me."

I felt elated about the closeness Julie now enjoys with God. It had been a long and painful journey for her. "Your life has changed dramatically, Julie. I'm so happy for you."

"I'm sometimes astounded to see how different my life is now. When God touched me, He changed my heart. My greatest desire is to share His love with others. I want to tell people about His forgiveness, grace, and mercy, and how He changed my life."

"God gave you the perfect opportunity to share your story during your church's praise night, didn't He?"

Julie paused as if reflecting on that night. "Perhaps God allowed me to speak as a blessing for turning to Him. God's love keeps growing deeper and wider inside me. His love and His Word have truly healed me from all the deep wounds of my past, especially the pain of my family name.

"Now I have peace and assurance that God and I will walk together forever. And He calls me by a new name: My daughter."

> I am leaving you with a gift—peace of mind and heart. And the peace I give is a gift the world cannot give. So don't be troubled or afraid. (John 14:27)

You can imagine how thrilled I was to hear about Julie's amazing encounter with Jesus, which brought her into a personal relationship with Him. And then, when Julie gave her personal testimony in church, she experienced God's healing from all her hurt, heartache, and rejection.

Julie had sought peace through people-pleasing and by ignoring her pain. She thought marrying and having children would bring her the peace and happiness she desired. But the rejection of divorce drove her deeper into despair.

Through all this, Julie discovered something we all need to know and believe: God is our only source of true peace. He knows our heartaches. Our sorrows. Our disappointments. Our fears. He knows everything in our minds and hearts that prevents us from experiencing peace and joy. God stands by our side, asking us to give Him our burdens so He can heal our hearts, rebuild our confidence, restore our hope, and give us His peace.

Julie let go of her self-condemnation, her heartache of rejection in relationships, and her fear of what people may think of her. When she allowed Jesus to lift those heavy burdens from her, she became free to bask in God's peace and presence.

> Then Jesus said, "Come to me, all of you who are weary and carry heavy burdens, and I will give you rest. Take my yoke upon you. Let me teach you, because I am humble and gentle at heart, and you will find rest for your souls. For my yoke is easy to bear, and the burden I give you is light." (Matthew 11:28–30)

The enemy doesn't want us to feel good about ourselves, feel accepted, or find peace for our souls. The enemy of God always lurks around the corner, waiting to defeat us by planting negative thoughts in our minds to rob us of peace.

Our gentle and loving Father, however, promises to give us the peace we desperately crave. We simply need to pray.

> Don't worry about anything; instead, pray about everything. Tell God what you need, and thank him for all he has done. Then you will experience God's peace, which exceeds anything we can understand. His peace will guard your hearts and minds as you live in Christ Jesus. (Philippians 4:6–7)

My Personal Prayer:

_____

_____

_____

_____

_____

_____

_____

_____

_____

_____

_____

Bible Memory Verse:

Then you will experience God's peace, which exceeds anything we can understand. His peace will guard your hearts and minds as you live in Christ Jesus. (Philippians 4:7)

Chapter Challenge:

- Think of a time when God brought peace to your heart when you most needed it. Write about the details, along with your thanks and praise to God.

_____

_____

_____

_____

- Do you struggle to forgive those who hurt you? Take some intentional time to list their names and ask God to take that burden from you and help you forgive each person. When you release them through forgiveness, you can be free from the power they had on you, especially whenever you remembered the hurt you experienced. Forgiveness will set you free.

_____

_____

_____

_____

- If God has changed your life, can you think of someone you'd like to tell your story to? Set aside time to invite them to your home or to meet in a nearby restaurant. Sharing your story might encourage them to share their own story with others.

_____

_____

_____

_____

Chapter 7

Shield of Faith
Denise Sanders

"**M**y mom's been married six times."

My friend Denise and I were in the middle of a pleasant walk near a lake when she confided this shocking truth about her mother. That weekend, we attended a women's retreat, which included small-group discussions. In our groups, we learned to identify our fear of rejection, acknowledge the defenses we'd built to keep others from knowing us, and let go of our defenses so God could set us free from fear.

I realized that Denise's surprise pronouncement about her mother was her way of divulging one of the reasons she grew up with a fear of rejection. Her admission took courage and trust, and it represented a huge step forward.

From what I had learned about Denise during the several years we'd been friends, I'd assumed she'd had a wonderful childhood. She easily loved people and always had a smile on her face. I'd seen her in action teaching and nurturing children and had observed her impact on those young lives.

I turned to Denise. "I would never have guessed you had this kind of homelife. After the retreat, I'd love to spend unhurried time together and learn more about your life. Want to come to my condo sometime?"

"I'd love to, Gail. I'm off on Fridays."

After we settled back into our routines, Denise and I agreed on a day and time. I looked forward to having her in my home, where we could talk freely.

Denise arrived at one o'clock as planned. I led her to my dining room table, which looked out on my patio and the refreshing scenery beyond. I prayed this setting would keep our spirits lifted while we talked about difficult topics.

"What a pretty home," she said. "This is perfect for you."

"I agree. Would you like a cold glass of water?"

"Sounds good." With a smile, she added, "I'll need it. I have a feeling I'll be talking the whole time."

I handed Denise her glass, and she settled into the soft mauve cushioned seat of one of the sturdy mahogany chairs I'd inherited from my grandmother.

After choosing a chair opposite her, opening my notepad, and taking a refreshing sip of water, I looked across the table at Denise's blond, curly hair and engaging smile. I found myself wondering how this sweet friend had survived the trauma she had hinted of.

"I have until four o'clock," Denise explained.

I smiled. We probably wouldn't need that much time.

Well, we did. Right up to four on the dot.

Behind the Scenes

Denise began. "My childhood was not normal. My mother hadn't grown up in a loving home, and she didn't know how to nurture her own children. Living in a small Kansas town, Mom and her oldest brother took care of their five siblings. Their mother—my grandmother—often beat them with a hairbrush. Because of the chaos at home, my mom wanted out. At the age of eighteen, she intentionally became pregnant so she could leave home.

"My mom's boyfriend, Rob, wanted to get married, so they did. Then eighteen months after I was born, my little brother, William, came along.

"My father worked evenings as a sheet-metal worker for the airline industry. As a hobby, he was a race car mechanic. My parents were married three years. She divorced him when I was two years old and William was six months. Many years later, William asked my mom why she divorced my dad. Her answer was, 'Because we didn't have a fairy-tale marriage.'

"I was only two, so I don't remember much about my father during that time. I'm grateful Mom gave me pictures of William and me with him and two pictures with only my dad and me, because they serve as memories of my childhood life with him. Fortunately, we would develop a close father-daughter relationship later."

Her mother had given her a precious gift. "I love that you have those keepsake pictures of your dad, and that you had a chance to reconnect."

"Many times, I thought I would never see him again. After the divorce, my mom rented a big, two-story house, most likely with my grandfather's financial help. My grandmother left him when I was young, and they divorced shortly after. During the day, Mom provided daycare in her home. Occasionally, I was aware of different men there in the evening, but I didn't know what that meant."

"What an unfortunate home environment, Denise. Did you feel your mother neglected you?"

"Mom didn't show us emotional love, for sure, but I don't remember her neglecting the daily things my brother and I needed."

Even though Denise and her brother, William, didn't have a loving home, they had each other. She described him as an adventurous, strong-willed brother.

"I remember the time William climbed out the upstairs window and walked around on the roof. A neighbor spotted him and told him to come down."

I shared a similar incident in my family. "When my brother was about six, he climbed up on our neighbor's roof. When he fell off, the neighbors saw him through the window and ran outside. The husband dashed to our house to tell our parents.

"My brother had gashed his cheek on a sharp rock in the garden, so my parents rushed him to the hospital. Greg needed stitches and was released with a large bandage on his face. Once they got home, my dad reprimanded him. His punishment soon ended, but the scar on Greg's face remained for life."

"Gail, it sounds as if we both had adventurous brothers."

A Different Scenario

Denise continued her story. "When I was six, my mom married her boyfriend, Jerry. He had two children but didn't have custody of them.

"Jerry was an alcoholic and physically abused William. I don't remember him hitting Mom or me, though.

"Two years later, Mom came home one day and found another woman with Jerry. She immediately filed for divorce, citing infidelity as the reason. I was eight years old and William was six and a half."

A Safe Place

Another upheaval for those two precious children. "Life was unpredictable for you. Did you have happy times too?"

"The happiest memories for William and me are the times we spent at our grandfather's farm near a small Kansas town. Our grandmother had already passed away. This grandfather, my mom's dad, became a father figure to us. He showed us unconditional love and provided spiritual nurturing. He is the reason I stayed tight with God and always went to church. I prayed and accepted Jesus at our church when I was five years old and was baptized later.

"My grandfather was aware of my mom's turbulent life. I think he may have felt like a failure because he couldn't prevent her from choosing that kind of lifestyle. I believe our visits to the farm were highlights for him and helped soften his sadness."

I pictured the three of them on the farm. "Did you get to see him often?"

"During the school year, my brother and I spent every other weekend with our grandfather. Each summer, we spent two or three weeks on the farm during harvest. I remember riding in my grandfather's truck and counting the cows.

"Instead of going to college and following his dream of becoming a pastor, my grandfather had stayed home and had taken over the family farm. It wasn't what he envisioned. However, I'll always be thankful that God used my grandfather to help William and me experience a calm and happy young life during our days on the farm."

I knew the importance of grandparents. "I'm thankful you had a wonderful grandfather to fill in the gaps. My grandmother is the one who always made me feel loved."

"William and I also enjoyed the times with our dad. He never lost connection with us. Once a month, he picked us up on a Saturday, and we spent the night at his house. The next morning, he brought us home. He had already remarried. Our stepmother, Marie, didn't make an effort to connect with us, but she seemed fine with our visits. One year, we all sat together in the living room and watched the Thanksgiving parade on TV."

The Saga Continues

"My mother's next boyfriend was Frank. She met him at a nightclub, and he eventually became her third husband. He had three children, ages fifteen, thirteen, and five. At that time, I was nine and William seven and a half.

"Mom and Frank liked to go dancing. Before they were married, he brought his three children to my mom's house prior to each dance. His two teenagers looked after the rest of us. When Mom and Frank got home, he gathered his three children and returned to his house."

"How did you feel about this arrangement?"

"Sad and lonely. I wanted to spend time with my mom, but instead, she left me alone and chose to go with Frank. She was still married at that time, but she'd already found another boyfriend. All this left William and me with conflicting emotions. We didn't know where we fit in. It had been just the three of us, but now she focused on this man and his three children.

"They got married the day after my mom's divorce from Jerry became final. Since Frank was in the military and lived at the base, we all moved there."

"What was it like to live on the base, Denise?"

"Our lives quickly changed. William and I were seldom allowed to visit our grandfather during the school year, and we no longer spent summers with him. I missed my grandfather's continual love and encouragement, and I started to feel empty inside.

"Also, Frank seemed to view his children as more important than William and me. For example, he didn't want to pay for my gymnastics, yet he paid his daughters' cheerleading expenses.

"Two years into the marriage, Frank was assigned to an air force base in England for three years. Before all of us left for England, Frank and my mom wanted to adopt each other's children. However, they hit a snag. For the adoptions to take place, our dad would have to relinquish his rights as our father."

I couldn't imagine what happened next.

"Mom tried to pave the way by fabricating a lie. She told our dad that he needed to give us up for adoption and allow Frank to adopt us because if we were hurt or became sick overseas, the military would not provide any treatment or medical assistance unless Frank was our legal guardian.

"My dad didn't seek legal counsel. He simply believed Mom. Later, my dad said he allowed the adoption because he couldn't be there, and this man would take care of us. He thought he was doing what was best for William and me."

"I'm glad you found out your dad's reason, Denise, but what did you think at the time?"

"I don't remember being emotional about it. William and I were excited about moving to England, so we went along with the plan. From what I understood, the adoption by Frank needed to happen so we could start our adventure in another country."

Denise's dad had no contact with her and William then, but perhaps everything would work out.

"One year after our arrival in England, Frank's mother passed away. Since his father was already in the early stages of dementia, and Frank was an only child, he was responsible for arranging the funeral. All of us flew stateside to his father's home."

Since Frank was his father's sole caregiver, he needed to get his dad a passport before he could go to England. This took time. Frank had to report back to duty at the military base by a certain date, so he took all five children back to England with him. Denise's mother stayed in the States for another month to help with the paperwork. When the passport was ready, Frank's father and Denise's mother traveled back to England.

A Devastating Shift

I wondered how Denise had dealt with the absence of her mother. "How did things work out once you got back?"

"As the middle child, I still felt left out, as I had before. Frank's son, Jacob, was eight, and my brother, William, was ten and a half. They played together and became friends for life. Frank's two daughters, Tina and Karen, were nineteen and eighteen, and they were close.

"I was twelve years old and about to enter seventh grade. Even though Rob was my real dad, Mom always said, 'Frank's your dad. You need to respect him and do what he says.' He seemed like a fine person, and I tried to obey. However, while my mom was still stateside, Frank became a different person. Or maybe his true self emerged in her absence. That was when the abuse began."

My heart beat faster.

"One early evening, when I was in my room, Frank's son, Jacob, knocked on my door and said, 'Dad wants you downstairs.'"

Denise explained what took place next. "I thought perhaps he wanted me to help his daughters cook dinner. I went downstairs and looked around but didn't see any activity. I decided to ask Frank. I walked down the hallway and saw the closed bedroom door.

"I knocked and heard him say, 'Come in.' As I opened the door, I saw him lying on the bed with no clothes on. He told me, 'Lie next to me.'

"I was horrified and afraid. Against all that was within me, I laid down with my clothes on. Next he said, 'Touch me.' Though repulsed, I did."

Denise doesn't remember how she got out of the room that night. "The only thing I do remember is his odor, which will haunt me the rest of my life. I blocked from my mind everything else that happened that night.

"The next day, Frank grounded me from calling my friends or spending time with them. I don't recall what reason he came up with. Thankfully, my mother returned to England soon after. I didn't tell her what had happened; that would come later."

I pushed my chair back and walked over to give Denise a hug. "Such an unthinkable, horrifying invasion into your young life."

I returned to my seat with a heavier heart.

Denise took a long drink as if she needed a break from remembering this trauma. "My mom worked in the mess hall for the GIs who lived in the barracks. She had to leave home early each morning while we kids were still asleep.

"Three different times after my mother left for work, Frank walked into my room and said, 'I wanted to make sure you heard your alarm.'"

Denise continued. "One morning before breakfast, Frank opened my door, but this time he climbed into bed with me. He touched and fondled me. My thin nightgown provided no protection. That was the worst time ever. He abused me two or three more days after my mother left for work."

I groaned. "I'm so sorry. You were defenseless."

"The next time my father walked into my room, woke me up, and began molesting me, something snapped inside. My brothers and sisters were still asleep. Eventually, they woke up, and I got dressed as usual.

"As soon as my father got dressed and left for work, I called my mom and told her what had happened that morning and the other times as well. She came home, bringing a military police officer with her. She told me, 'I believe you, and I want to take action.'

"Another officer went to dad's work and brought him back to the house. When the two officers confronted my dad about the abuse, he denied it."

I asked, "Since he denied it, was that the end?"

Denise said, "No, there's more. Two days later, he and my mom and I were called in for counseling at the base. The male counselor looked at me and said, 'You are promiscuous. What did you say to invite him into your bedroom? What were you wearing?'

"Then the counselor told me to sit knee to knee with my dad, facing him. I felt sick to my stomach. Then the counselor told me to say to my father, 'I love you and I'm sorry.'

"Abruptly, my mom stood. Without a word, she took my hand and rushed me home. Dad returned on his own. The next day, Mom quit her job so she could stay home."

I wondered if that provided enough protection for Denise.

A Potential Escape

"I still felt fearful. Many times, I begged my mom to send me to her father's farm. 'Grandpa will take care of me. I'll be safe there.'

"Whenever I asked her, she always responded, 'I have to stay here. His children need me.' Since the threat of Frank's abuse remained, I couldn't understand why she wouldn't let me leave. In my heart, her actions confirmed my fears: she cared more about herself and his children than she cared about me and my safety.

"After I pestered her for a year and a half, Mom announced to William and me, 'I'm leaving Frank. The three of us are moving home to live with Uncle Scott in Orlando.' I had no idea why she waited so long to leave Frank, when she'd had many other opportunities to do so. Later, I would discover she didn't intend to leave him. She and Frank had worked out a plan for all of us to live together in the US."

Shortened Freedom

Trying to keep up with the drama, I asked, "So the three of you left England. What was happening with Frank and the military?"

"The military had been watching him since our earlier counseling session. My mother, William, and I returned to the US in the summer of that year, and in November, the military told Frank, 'If you retire, your records will be sealed. Otherwise, we plan to dishonorably discharge you.'

"I was not surprised that he chose to retire so no one would ever know about the abuse. But the fact that the military forced my dad to leave brought me some relief, because I saw it as proof that they believed my story."

I was grateful that Denise could at least walk away from her horrible experiences in England.

"When I was thirteen and a half and William was twelve, Frank left England with his son, Jacob, and his daughter Karen. Tina had already left home. The three of them moved to Orlando, the city where we lived with Uncle Scott. That made me nervous because I didn't know Frank's intentions.

"As I said, Mom never told us ahead of time that all six of us would live together in a big house in Orlando. I discovered the plan through conversations I overheard. I felt betrayed."

I assured Denise, "I would have felt the same way."

"I saw pure selfishness on their part," she said. "After feeling safe here, with Frank in England, I was now forced to live with him again without having any say in the matter. I was agitated and scared, and I felt sick inside. I went into survival mode, asking myself, 'What should I expect? What's going to happen to me?' With no one to talk to, I buried my fear inside."

Renewed Fear

"I had my own room at the front of our one-story house. Only sheer curtains hung at the full-length window. As I recall, Mom chose those curtains.

"Fortunately, my dad no longer abused me inside our house. However, he was free to walk to the front yard any time he wanted and look in my bedroom window. Fear rose up in me.

"I wasn't allowed to lock my bedroom door. So each night, as I closed my door, I slid a butter knife between the door jamb and the door so Frank couldn't come in. Because of my sheer curtains, I always changed clothes inside my closet with the door closed."

For sure, Denise became a helpless victim again. A prisoner in her own home.

She told me how God provided hope of protection for her during that time. "I regularly babysat for a pastor and his wife who lived nearby. When I told them about my father's abuse, they told me, 'If you ever feel unsafe going home at night, you can stay here in our spare room.' I took them up on their offer several times.

"The pastor and his wife wanted to help by reporting the abuse to the authorities, but since I had no substantial proof that he was looking in my window, we had nothing to report. It would be my word against his.

"From tenth grade through twelfth grade, I lived with sheer curtains and the uncertainty of whether my dad watched me through the window."

A New Era

"I hoped something would change after high school. Following graduation, my brother and I heard that our church was organizing a mission trip to Guatemala. We both wanted to go. Surprisingly, Mom and Frank allowed us to join the group. We had to come up with the money, which we did by creating a fundraiser.

"Once overseas, we had a thrilling time, meeting many young people and serving in the Guatemalan church. At the end of the week, it was hard to say goodbye, but we never forgot those experiences. They represented a peaceful time in our lives."

Their mom met them at the Orlando airport, but she gave them unsettling news.

"As soon as Mom spotted us, her face red and her eyes flashing, she announced, 'I'm leaving Frank. We're going back to the house to get your stuff, and then we're moving to the apartment I've already rented.'

"I felt betrayed again. Many times, she could have left Frank and saved me from his abuse. Why did she decide to leave only now, when I would soon leave home? How selfish and uncaring of her.

"I thought about all the times Frank had abused me inside our house in England and most likely stalked me from outside our home in the States. As I listened to my mother ranting about Frank, all I could think was, *You're leaving Frank because he's threatening to hurt you for the first time. But you sacrificed me by not rescuing me from his abuse.* My resentment toward my mom became one more hurt I buried deep."

My heart broke for Denise because she had no way to undo the trauma and devastation she experienced both in England and the US.

Denise continued, "William and I went with Mom to the apartment she'd rented. However, a year later, when I was nineteen and William seventeen, my mom decided to leave both of us and move to Gainesville for her new job. She rented a room for me from a divorced woman with a child. She placed William with a family in the church."

I couldn't hold back my words. "That's abandonment on top of abuse, Denise. How did you manage? Or was it better without your mom?"

"It seemed strange without her," Denise said, "but I didn't miss the chaos. It was the beginning of freedom for me in some ways, because I didn't have to know about her life or be concerned for her.

"Eventually, I learned that Gary, the man who hired her for the job in Gainesville, had become her fourth husband. He later died in a car crash.

"Mom's fifth husband, Juan, was a drug addict who ended up taking everything from my mother, leaving her penniless. By that time, I was married to Stephen. Fortunately, before we were married, I told Stephen all about my childhood experiences and Frank's abuse. Later, I told him of my mother's escapades as I learned about each new husband."

With my curiosity at a high, I said, "What was Stephen's response to your mother's latest crisis?"

"Actually, he wasn't shocked. We immediately discussed how we could help her. As a strong Christian man with an understanding and caring heart, Stephen agreed to open our home to her. During those unexpected two years of having my mother in our home, Stephen and I learned how far God's grace could stretch.

"When my mom was on her feet again financially, she left our home. Not long afterward, she met and eventually married David, husband number six. When I met David, he seemed like a great guy and a gentle person. He was lonely, since his children lived with his ex-wife. David and Mom got along well, and he's good with finances. I began hoping and praying they would stay together, and I still pray for that."

Fulfillment of a Dream

I could hardly comprehend the trauma Denise endured throughout the years, with many fathers and much abuse. I was thankful she hung on to God.

"Denise, would you like to take a break and walk around my complex?"

"Let's do," she said. "Now that I've told you about my six fathers, we can talk about happier times."

The outside air felt great—sunny with a soft breeze. A couple of neighbors passed us with their dogs. Denise and I bent down to pet them both. One of my favorite little neighbor boys whizzed by on his scooter, and I waved. His smile always cheered me up.

Once we were settled back inside, I asked, "What was your life like after you graduated from high school?"

"I always wanted to be a teacher, so I had my eyes set on college. My dilemma, though, was funds. I needed Frank to sign my application papers for a student loan and a Pell grant from the military. He refused.

"Although I couldn't attend college, my dream of teaching remained. God knew my heart for children. I got a job as a substitute teacher in the elementary school my church sponsored. That became my first step in God's full plan for me.

"I eventually began teaching full time, and my ministry kept expanding. I currently teach the Bible to the children in our church school during the week and in kids' church on Sundays. Each Sunday morning, I deliver a children's sermon during our services, which I've found impacts not only the children, but the adults as well."

I'm proud of all Denise has achieved while pursuing her dream. "Your life and expanding ministry is inspiring, Denise. Tell me more."

"Today, I'm the children's ministry director at my church, which allows me to oversee everything that happens with our children.

"Four years ago, I became a licensed pastor, which to me is the culmination of everything God had in mind for me. I couldn't go to college and become an elementary teacher as I had dreamed, but God gave me something better. My ministry with the children in church, which includes children from the community, is not merely a job. It's a wonderful opportunity to speak into the lives of children from birth through fifth grade, not just teach one class in an elementary school."

I sat there in awe of all God had done. "It's fascinating to see how God fulfilled an even bigger dream for you. Now you can minister to many children and even their parents."

Interests of the Heart

"God also fulfilled my desire to be married," she said. "Let me back up and tell you how that happened. At the beginning of my involvement with the children at church, I met Stephen. He had graduated from a local trade school and became a certified mechanic. Stephen worked nights at the church, where he was in charge of security. He also set up the fellowship hall for events during the week and arranged individual rooms for meetings and conferences as needed.

"At the end of my work day as a teacher, I often crossed paths with Stephen before he began his evening work. We dated for a year while attending the young adult class together. We dated for months before we had our first kiss.

"I was shocked when Stephen proposed to me. Because of everything that had happened in my life, I didn't think I was marriage material. But God gave me faith to say yes. Later, Stephen said he didn't think I'd marry him. When I asked why, he said, 'I didn't think I was marriage material.'"

Denise and I laughed about the coincidence. "Your long marriage proves you were meant for each other. But you were hesitant, so what changed your mind?"

"Steven's parents were the reason I had confidence to say yes. I felt especially close to his mother. She became an influential person in my life.

"Stephen and I were engaged for eleven months before we got married. The best part of our wedding was my grandfather walking me down the aisle and giving me away, thirty-two years ago."

With joy, I said to Denise, "I can imagine the big smile on your loving grandfather's face."

"Stephen and I had big smiles too. We were delighted with the birth of our first child, Elaina, three years later. When she was six months old, I began substitute teaching at the church. Stephen's father and mother watched her during the day.

"Over the years, God blessed us with two more daughters and a son. The happiness we feel as a close and loving family has been a wonderful gift to Stephen and me."

Denise passed a family picture across the table. As I saw the way they hugged, I knew they loved each other. "Denise, your family's happiness is God's wonderful redemption for you."

Path to Redemption

"Yes, and I want to tell you another way God redeemed my life after all my trauma. When we moved to England, my real dad and I lost track of each other. After we moved to Orlando, I wanted to reconnect with him, but I didn't know how to reach him. In reality, my mom knew his phone number in Kansas, but she withheld that information from me for fourteen years. By then, I was already married."

The depth of cruelty and selfishness stunned me. "That's unimaginable. What happened after that?"

"When she finally told me how to contact my dad, I decided to write him a letter and ask him to visit me. I explained I didn't know how to reach him before, but now I hoped we could see each other.

"He called me, and within a week he came to Florida. He and my stepmother stayed for a week at a hotel near Disney. Stephen and I, along with our two children, went there every day. We swam in the pool and sang karaoke downstairs in the evenings. One of the highlights of my dad and Marie's visit was celebrating my daughter Emily's second birthday party with him at our home.

"The last day before he returned to Kansas, he took me aside. With sober eyes, he said, 'I'm so sorry I left you with that man. I thought he would take care of you as I would have taken care of you. I'm responsible for your abuse.'"

Hearing those tender and caring words from Denise's dad pierced my heart. Her dad couldn't undo the terrible things that happened to his daughter, but the love he poured into her in those moments must have changed her life. "Incredible, Denise. How did you respond?"

"Through my tears, I told him I did not hold him responsible for Frank's actions. When we hugged, I was overwhelmed with emotion. While I felt joyful, I also wished we could spend more time together.

"I was amazed he knew about my abuse. He said my uncle had told him. My dad and uncle were best friends in high school and stayed connected through mutual friends. I assume my mom told my uncle what had happened to me.

"After my dad and I reconnected in Orlando, we called each other often and visited each other's families every other year."

I looked across the table at the glow on her face. "Finally, a full circle for the two of you. I'm wondering about your brother, William. Did he have a chance to reconnect with your dad, too?"

"At the time my dad came to visit me in Orlando, William was in the military and stationed in Europe. After he returned stateside, he was able to reconnect with our dad. They visited each other once in a while, but were unable to create a close bond.

"William and I have always been close. We went through all our traumatizing years together. Even after being on our own, we have kept in touch. William now works in the aeronautical industry. His career has taken him out of the country, and also moved him out of state, but we stay connected."

The Real Story

Denise then revealed some behind-the-scenes details about the search for her father. "When my biological father, Rob, died twelve years ago, I flew to Kansas for his funeral. There my aunt told me, 'When your dad learned from your uncle that you were back in the States, he used two weeks of vacation time from work to look for you in Florida. But he couldn't find you.'

"I was shocked. Tears trickled down my face. I felt a deep sadness that he hadn't found me at that time and that we didn't connect earlier.

I wished I'd had more time with my dad.

"My aunt continued, 'Your dad and uncle connected in Florida, but your uncle told him you lived in the southern part of the state. In those days, it wasn't easy to track people down, so he couldn't find you.'"

Denise confided in me, "Somehow, I knew my mom had told my uncle to lie to my dad so he wouldn't find me. I became angry that she would even think of doing that to me. The emotions of yet another betrayal consumed me."

I could hardly bear the thought of another betrayal for Denise.

"A couple of years later, God told me I had to forgive my mother. After wrestling and searching my heart, I knew He was right. I had to forgive her before I could heal emotionally. That was the only way I could move on with my life. With God's help, I forgave my mother for preventing my father from finding me in Florida, for allowing me to stay in the abusive situation with Frank in England, and for intentionally moving me back into the house with Frank in the US, even with the threat of his abuse.

"When I forgave my mother as God desired me to do, the Lord set me free from past resentment and helped me begin to live in freedom from my mother's control."

I admired Denise's courage. "Your willingness to forgive her released you to walk in freedom on your new path."

"You're so right," she said. "Many people have supported me and helped me keep moving forward on this new journey. I stopped crumbling under my old thoughts, like, 'What will my mom think of this?' or 'What will she do when she hears this?'

"After a certain incident with my mother, one of my friends told me, 'It's on your mom.' Her words helped me see the truth that not everything is my fault."

A valuable insight for Denise to apply in her healing.

"After hearing that truth, I've stopped wrestling with every issue, believing I need either to solve it and resolve it or shrink back and apologize. Instead, I'm learning to let go of the familiar pull of always considering what my mom might say or do. My responsibility is to deal only with my part of the circumstance or situation. Embracing this new perspective and forgiving my mother has enabled me to disengage myself from her so I can stand strong as my own person.

"My mother will probably never admit that all the things that happened tore me up, but that doesn't matter anymore. God knows everything I went through. He rescued me and has redeemed my life through the joy I now experience with my own family and my ministry with children.

"God is my shield. He protects my mind and heart each day. I want to continue to live by faith and follow God's leading on my new path of freedom."

> But you, O LORD, are a shield around me; you are my glory,
> the one who holds my head high. (Psalm 3:3)

God rescued Denise from a life of trauma and helped her break free. He shields her and gives her grace, wisdom, and courage to deal with each situation she encounters on her new journey. Denise once lived in fear, caused by the people who hurt her. Her past ruled her thoughts and actions. Now she lives with new confidence as a strong woman who has become an influencer, especially with children.

One of the most significant decisions Denise made was to forgive her mother for the ways she hurt her. Unforgiveness keeps us in bondage to the person who hurt us. Forgiveness sets us free from the power they had over us.

By not forgiving a person, we allow what they did to consume our thought life. We keep reliving the way they hurt us.

Some people withhold their forgiveness because they mistakenly believe that, if they extend forgiveness, they're saying the person's actions were all right. The truth is, forgiving doesn't excuse the person's behavior. Rather, we acknowledge that they've hurt us in some way, but we're willing to forgive.

Others withhold forgiveness because they think they can punish the offender that way. In reality, they harm only themselves. Without forgiveness, they're still bound to the other person and overpowered by thoughts of the offense.

Forgiving allows us to detach from the offender. It releases us from dwelling on what the person did and recycling the details through our minds. Occasionally, we may recall what happened, but even that brief thought will no longer overpower us. Forgiveness sets us free to move forward.

Denise felt betrayed by her mother and enslaved by her dominance. Denise's willingness to forgive her mother for the past enabled her to let go of her mother's power over her. Now, when she realizes her focus has shifted back to her mother's opinions, she releases those thoughts to God and asks Him to keep her focused on Him so she can make progress on her journey of freedom.

The enemy wants to keep us imprisoned by the actions of others. However, if we belong to God, we have His power inside us to resist the enemy's strategies. By relying on the Lord's power, we can keep forgiving others who hurt us, and we can stay strong and focused on Him. We can live the abundant and free life God promised if we continually put on God's spiritual armor that protects our minds and hearts.

> In addition to all [parts of God's armor], hold up the shield of faith to stop the fiery arrows of the devil. (Ephesians 6:16)

My Personal Prayer:

_____

_____

_____

_____

_____

_____

_____

_____

_____

_____

Bible Memory Verse:

Walk by faith, not by sight. (2 Corinthians 5:7 NASB)

Chapter Challenge:

- Have you ever experienced trauma? What was it? If you have hesitated to share that part of your life with a counselor or trusted friend, ask God for courage to seek out someone who can help you process your experience. When you expose your experiences to the light of God, you weaken the power those experiences have over you.

  _____

  _____

  _____

  _____

  _____

- Read Ephesians 6:10–18, which explains the full armor God has given us. Each day, verbally put on your spiritual armor, including the shield of faith. Journal your thoughts about this armor helping you feel safe and secure against the enemy's accusations.

  _____

  _____

  _____

  _____

  _____

- Seek out a Christian friend who feels weak and discouraged because of their past. Encourage them by sharing Isaiah 43:18–19 or another Bible verse that will help them let go of their past. Call them, get together, mail a card, or text or email the verses to them.

Chapter 8

No Longer a Puzzle
Carmen Rivera

"When I was three years old, my father left, and fear of rejection wound itself around my heart."

When my friend Carmen spoke these words during our lunch date, I wanted to cry my heart out. I knew some of her story, but I had no idea of the trauma that began at such an early age.

Carmen and I first crossed paths four years ago during a book signing at a popular arts festival in Orlando. The sun was bright as always, so my author friends and I were grateful for the small tent that shaded us. We arranged our books and bookmarks on the long table as creatively as we could to capture the attention of passersby.

While standing with my friends, I noticed a young woman perusing my book *Life Through Loss: Facing Your Pain, Finding Your Purpose*.

Drawing closer, I smiled when she lifted her eyes.

"This book is for me," she said. "My mother died one week ago."

I placed my hand on her shoulder. "I know about your pain. My mother died too."

Our hearts connected. I signed a book for her and suggested we take a picture together. That encounter blossomed into friendship.

The Story Unfolds

A couple of weeks later, after capturing her email from the list of those who had purchased my book, I sent her a message. "Would you like to meet for lunch sometime?"

Immediately, Carmen suggested we meet at Perkins the following Saturday.

We met in the parking lot and exchanged a hug. "I'm glad we could meet on this free day from our offices," I said.

At our request, our greeter directed us to a booth in the corner. As we settled in, I observed Carmen's natural beauty and grace. When our server arrived, I asked for my favorite tomato-basil soup and an almond-chicken-salad sandwich. Carmen ordered a bowl of potato soup and lemonade.

When we were alone, I said, "How are you doing? I know you miss your mom."

"I still can't believe she's gone. We were so close. You know us Latinos—it's all about family. However, my biggest emotional support came from the caring words of my special girlfriends.

"My father's traumatic rejection filled me with fear of abandonment. I lived the next forty-seven years of my life trying to please people because I thought their approval would give me security. I sought love and ended up with the wrong person. I desperately looked for anything I thought would fill my empty life. Food and material things became obsessions.

"My intense goal of pleasing others caused me to feel as if I were locked in a box and couldn't breathe. I had no freedom to move up or down, right or left.

"I didn't like my bound-up life, but keeping others happy mattered most. My happiness intertwined with their happiness. This unrealistic goal twisted into a vicious cycle, leaving me drained. I never stood up for myself or allowed myself to be honest with others, and that fact haunted me."

"Carmen, I understand the stress of trying to please everyone, because that's what I did. I agree; it's a vicious cycle because we never succeed."

Our server chose that moment to deliver our drinks and steaming bowls of soup. After enjoying our soup on that chilly day, I asked Carmen to tell me more about her early life.

Searching for Significance

"I grew up on the small island of Puerto Rico with my mother and three siblings, Ivelisse, Lisette, and Manuel.

"When I look back, I see my humble beginnings. My mom, a single mother of four, worked hard throughout her life to provide food and necessities for us. Being the youngest, I learned to settle for less and to appreciate the little things in life.

"My life was simple but happy. I loved visiting my grandmother on Sundays. Getting together as a family during a hurricane represented safety, caring, and closeness to me.

"We had joyful times too—playing with siblings and competing in board games with my mom. My school friends and I spent a lot of time talking about girl things. I also hung out with my nearby cousins and looked forward to them staying with me in our home during weekends."

"What about your teen years?"

"I remember feeling grown up at fifteen, when I worked as a supermarket cashier. Apart from work and school, life centered around enjoying the culture and the wonderful food. And laughing at absolutely anything. We had a lot of happy days."

I was glad for her pleasant memories, but I wondered if Carmen's early fear of rejection still gripped her at times. "How did the memory of your father's abandonment affect you as a teenager?"

"Fear of rejection still paralyzed me. But I knew the rest of my family and my friends loved and accepted me. That helped fill my heart.

"Sadly, I was not the only one in our family who suffered from the fear of rejection. My mother struggled with her own fears. Both her mother and her husband—my father—had abandoned her. Out of sadness for her, I made it my responsibility to bring joy and to care for her as much as I could.

"I have no doubt that I allowed codependency to grow, relying on my mother to love and encourage me and allowing her to become a father figure to fill the empty space in my life. In my teenage years, I learned that my codependency prevented me from branching out and becoming my own person."

Source of Shame

This happens often in one-parent homes. "Carmen, I understand that your codependency formed because only your mother was there for you from the age of three."

"Right. It was good that my mother and I could help each other, but she faced the disgrace society put on her as a single mother with four children. Our homelife became a source of shame for me as well.

"My desperate desire to be accepted by others haunted me throughout my teenage years. I saw other young people who were blessed with a complete family, including a father who was the head of the household—something I never experienced."

I could identify with her. My father didn't abandon me at an early age, but my parents divorced. Whenever my college friends talked about their parents and all the fun things they did as a family, my heart filled with pain and regret.

"Carmen, I understand a little about the shame you felt from being raised by a single mother. My parents divorced when I was thirteen. I felt ashamed of my broken family, and I didn't tell anyone except my best friend. Like you, I believed I'd missed out on having a normal family—a complete family. You suffered, but I'm grateful you had a mother who loved you."

"My mother filled many gaps in my life during those years, but my father's abandonment still created a ball of fear whenever I pondered my future life."

Future Vision

"I remember being determined to have a big family of my own one day and to give my future children the presence and love of a father. My dream of a perfect family pushed me to take control of my life."

I was fascinated with Carmen's next words. "I created a visual puzzle in my mind to figure out what I needed to do to experience a perfect life. I convinced myself that my main task in life was to put each piece of the puzzle in the right place. Then my dream of a perfect life would eventually become reality and match the picture on the front of the box."

"I can see your intensity in striving for your dream of a perfect life, Carmen, even at your young age."

A Big Step

"You're right. I kept my eyes on my dream. But when I was seventeen, my mother decided to move us to Bridgeport, Connecticut, where my two sisters lived. My oldest sister, Ivelisse, was stationed there in the army. Lisette held a permanent job with the federal government in Bridgeport, where she'd moved a year before we arrived. Once my mom and I settled in Bridgeport, Lisette moved into our new house with us."

"How did you feel about your mother's plan?"

"Inside, I fought the idea because I was scared to leave Puerto Rico. But the only way to finish my life puzzle was to give in to my mother's desire to move. She thought we would have a better life in the US.

"Also, because my mother had some differences with my brother and his future wife, she wanted a change. When we moved to Bridgeport, my brother, Manuel, stayed on the island. We kept in touch with him, but the relationship between Manuel and my mother remained strained. I was pleased that Manuel attended my wedding later."

I viewed this as a huge upheaval for Carmen's family personally and financially. "I'm curious how God enabled that major move to take place."

"My mother owned her home on the island. She sold it and had enough to support the two of us in Connecticut.

"We arrived in Bridgeport in the summer of 1985. I had only a high school diploma, had no skills, and hardly spoke English. I wondered what lay ahead for me."

Those seemed like impossible obstacles to overcome. "What a drastic change for you. At least you were with your mom and sisters."

"Being a part of a family provided the emotional support I needed. However, it was challenging to begin my adult life in a different country. Everything was new to me, from the language to the culture to the weather."

"At least you had your high school diploma," I said. "But how did you manage in those early days?"

"Living in another culture and learning a new language was extremely hard. I felt ashamed and different from the rest of the people in this country. I didn't speak much English, and my accent was so heavy, people used to laugh at my pronunciation."

Carmen said she carried a Spanish/English dictionary everywhere she went. "I made myself learn the meaning of many words each day. I was determined to learn the language and not accept support from the government or other people, as some Latinos did.

"Mom registered me for English as a second language classes in a junior college. When the classes didn't help much, I decided to purchase an English program and work online."

Carmen's perseverance amazed me. It seemed as if she kept pushing obstacles aside.

"I wanted to enroll in Butler Business School with all English classes. I remember not having the money to pay for the school and asking my dad to assist me. He refused to help, so I applied for a student loan. That loan enabled me to complete my schooling."

Moving Forward

"While studying at Butler, I secured several jobs. I cleaned a doctor's office at night, typed settlement statements at a real estate office, and worked as a cashier at a supermarket. I was engaged in all these jobs simultaneously without knowing much English.

"Going to school and working in different positions became enjoyable because I grew in my confidence and learned new skills."

"Even with the challenges you faced, Carmen, you achieved two significant results."

"I'm grateful. After finishing my classes at the business school, I decided to take some data entry courses, which I also completed. With all these courses under my belt, I worked in a few offices as a temporary employee.

"All these experiences landed me a job as a data entry clerk in a travel agency. Being a data entry clerk was easy for me, since I didn't have to communicate much with others.

"I literally learned English through the junior college, the business school, and the offices. My willingness to learn English became my greatest advantage."

I told Carmen, "I can't express my admiration for you enough, after hearing about your unfailing determination to learn the language, fit in with the culture, and work in various positions."

"Thank you, Gail. I wanted to fit in and also have a good life here. But my past rejection affected my life, even as an adult. All my life, I'd carried the burden of rejection and fear on my shoulders because of my father's abandonment."

Carmen added, "That imaginary backpack felt heavier each day. But I pushed aside personal thoughts and convinced myself I could still have control of my life. All I needed was to continue placing more pieces in my puzzle, such as getting married, having a career, buying a home, and having a happy family.

"I put a piece in place when I was offered my first permanent job as a data entry clerk. Another piece fit in my puzzle when I cared for my mother in her sickness and helped my siblings."

A Decision

"Carmen, what about your desire to be married and raise a family?"

"I still clung to my hope of having a loving husband. Just like that, I met a man I thought was the one. I believed Dean would take away my feelings of rejection and provide the personal protection I'd missed all my life. He would fill me with confidence, happiness, and love. He'd see my uniqueness—the real me—and he would love and accept me as I was."

Those descriptions created the same hope in me as Carmen seemed to be feeling. "How did you meet Dean and what attracted you to him?"

"We met in a club. I didn't want to go with my friends that night, but they pushed me to join them. My friends invited Dean and his friend to join our table. Dean sat next to me and we connected easily. Before the evening was over, we'd set up a time to meet again.

"We began spending all our free time together. We dated for a year before getting married at the age of twenty. Now I realize I got married in order to gain independence, but I also truly thought Dean was my happiness.

"Two days after our wedding, we moved to Ashland, Massachusetts, where we lived in a rented apartment for two and a half years. Once we became more financially stable, we purchased a town house in Easton, Massachusetts, and lived there for the next three and a half years. We were basically on our own, since neither of our families had homes nearby."

I wondered how her family felt about Dean.

"After I married Dean," she said, "my father visited us in Massachusetts every summer. Even though he abandoned me when I was three years old, Dad's choice to be involved in my new life began to heal our relationship. We became so close that I offered to donate one of my kidneys to him when he was sick.

"Since we had limited finances at the beginning, Dean and I spent most of our free time together in our apartment. We enjoyed cooking together. We also liked going to parks, driving around town, and spending time with friends. Later, when our finances stabilized, we visited family in Connecticut and traveled to other parts of Massachusetts.

"Marrying at an early age was not easy. Unfortunately, I brought along old baggage from my life in Puerto Rico and from rejection in my new country."

Many of us know how damaging old baggage can be. God wants us to let go of our past and move forward so we can be a part of His present and future plans for us. However, that takes time.

"Many aspects of being a wife challenged me," Carmen confided, "but those difficulties mingled with my happy days with Dean."

"I'm glad you had happy times with Dean. But I can tell the weight of your rejection remained in your mind and heart."

"I still felt that weight, but I focused on maintaining control of all aspects of my life every day. Outwardly, I welcomed challenges. But inside, my determination to succeed in everything became my worst enemy, because nothing measured up to my expectations, including my marriage."

The Collapsing Plan

I thought about everything Carmen juggled. "You carried a lot of responsibility in many areas of your life. How did your marriage fail to measure up to your expectations?"

"With the passing of years, my husband and I faced career, financial, and relationship challenges. Throughout our marriage, Dean held multiple jobs. Our finances were a mess because we didn't know how to manage our money. Our relationship fell apart because Dean's emotions continually fluctuated.

"During our marriage, Dean's mother developed cancer and died. Soon after that, his father also developed cancer and died. Dean felt alone, and his sadness and depression grew.

"Without family nearby, we struggled. The cold weather made

us depressed. Many times, I suggested we move south to Florida. We would, but later."

"Were you both still working?"

"Yes. In fact, we both worked for a successful temporary agency. Our careers blossomed, but for me, something was missing. We wanted to have children, but I struggled to become pregnant."

Although I'd never faced the heartache of infertility, I knew couples who faced enormous stress when they couldn't have the children they dreamed of. I could understand how that inability would increase Carmen's sense of rejection.

"Infertility raged as a battle within me. My uncooperative body kept me in bondage to my feelings of rejection and fear. Relying on assistance from a fertility doctor became personal shame. Rejection haunted me day and night and broke down my sense of control.

"I still clung to hope. While continuing my prayers for a child, I kept placing other puzzle pieces here and there. I thought, 'Surely when I finish my puzzle, I'll feel complete and have a happy life.'"

Fortunately, the server came our way with her coffee pot. I was more than ready for a refill and a reason to take a break from these sad issues my friend had faced. With our refreshed coffee cups in hand, we both turned to the window, bathing in the rays of sunshine and welcoming the sight of healthy greenery, a confirmation that God's creation is alive and well, even when our lives take a dive.

Clamoring for More

I agonized with Carmen's inability to become pregnant—the one thing she couldn't control. I prayed for Carmen as she continued her story.

"In the midst of the circumstances swirling around me, I managed to convince myself that purchasing a home and working harder on my career would somehow fill my empty heart.

"Dean and I moved to Florida in December 1994. We rented out our town house in Easton, Massachusetts. In Orlando, we leased an apartment first and eventually built our own house. During this time, my career expanded. In January 1995, I began work as a legal assistant for a title insurance company. From legal assistant, I was promoted to paralegal after I completed my necessary classes."

"You continue to amaze me, Carmen. You undoubtedly deserved your promotion."

"Thank you. Meanwhile, our family shifted a bit. In 1997, my brother Manuel decided to join us in Orlando, and I helped him get settled. Soon my oldest sister, Ivelisse, who had been living in North Carolina, moved to Orlando with her two sons. Later, my mother moved from Bridgeport to Orlando, and my other sister, Lisette, transferred to a Miami office. However, she didn't like it there and moved back to Connecticut."

Since family meant so much to Carmen, I was happy that many of them were together.

Carmen then told me more about her job. "After years of working for the title insurance company, I realized God was showing me this was the career I could grow in and become successful. Unfortunately, I was so determined to advance my career, I became a slave to money. The more money I made, the more I wanted. This meant I was also a slave to my work as I focused on my strengths and strove to excel even more.

"But I wanted people to like me too, so I also became enslaved to the people at work and even my husband. At home, I stayed in my husband's shadow. I knew his favorite color and his favorite food, but he didn't know mine."

Motherhood at Last

"During this time, what was happening with your desire for a child?"

"After four years of fertility treatments and many prayers, an important puzzle piece fell into place. I became a mother. I gave birth to a beautiful son, and we named him Michael."

"Finally, a bright spot, Carmen."

"Michael did brighten our lives. I truly thought having a child would deepen our marriage and bring us closer."

"Did you see a difference in your marriage?"

"Unfortunately not. In fact, I began to see a different side of Dean I hadn't noticed before. He always viewed everything negatively and argued with me whenever I presented an idea. Nothing and no one were good enough. From his viewpoint, he was never to blame for bad things that happened to him. They were all someone else's fault.

"Whenever I wanted to discuss parenting issues, he never wanted to engage in that kind of conversation. He did spend time with the baby at first, but then he began refusing to play outside with Michael and me. He slid into a depression that lasted for years. I never knew Dean didn't want to be a father until after we had divorced years later.

"As I think back on our life together, I don't think Dean was ever happy in our marriage. Something inside prevented him from showing me his real self. Dean chased control, money, and power. He came from broken parents who didn't live together. They couldn't model a strong relationship because his mother was 'the other woman.' Dean's father was married and had a family."

I felt sad about the obstacles that prevented Carmen from enjoying her life as a wife and mother.

All Alone

"Describe more about your life after Michael was born."

"Being a parent gave me many happy moments. Unconditional love flowed from my heart as I spent time with my beautiful son. Yet I was overwhelmed with being a mother, working a full-time job, and taking care of our home. At one point, I took care of our finances too, which heightened my stress. I lived in fear that, at any time, my husband would tell me he'd quit his job or was going to find another job because he was unhappy.

"Knowing my life wasn't as it should be, I decided to wear an invisible mask to hide my pain and shame from others. I didn't want anyone to know the burden I carried. By hiding, I hoped both the world and my child would think I was fearless and confident and that rejection was no longer a part of my life."

My heart broke. I was familiar with trying to cover up my feelings. "I understand your desire to hide your life from others. You were doing the best you could, considering everything you had to juggle. I wish a friend could have come alongside you and supported you."

"That would have been wonderful, but I didn't want anyone to know," she said.

Loss of a Dream

Carmen related more discoveries. "I noticed changes in Dean after Michael was born, but I tried to focus on work and home and to keep going. Dean and I wrestled with usual marriage issues, but I knew his behavior went much deeper. I didn't know what to do.

"When Michael was eight years old, everything crumbled. In the early afternoon on Friday, December 21, 2007, an email popped up on my screen. It was Dean, saying he wanted out of our marriage."

I couldn't believe he sent that news through an email. "How shocking, Carmen. What were your thoughts?"

"Prior to receiving his email, I suspected infidelity with a coworker he used to take night classes with. I discovered an email between them and, of course, questioned him. He denied it, yelling at me for checking his email.

"Now I couldn't believe the message in front of me. I read it over and over, scrambling to decide my next move. Feelings of sadness and rejection bombarded me. I felt confused and out of control. I screamed at God because I couldn't understand what I had done to deserve the pain speeding through me and the rejection my son would experience."

"What happened next?"

"I knew Dean would ask for an official divorce, but I expected it to come after Christmas. However, he verbally asked for a divorce on December 21, the same day he sent me the email.

"Because it was four days before Christmas, and Dean still lived in our house, I figured I could at least keep the news from my son and make this last Christmas special for him. Also, out-of-town family would soon arrive, and I didn't want them to discover that Dean wanted a divorce."

"How did you even survive the holiday, Carmen?"

"Part of me loved him, but part of me knew his infidelity would not stop. He wanted to stay, but I had uncovered more details about this coworker, including the fact that he still communicated with her.

"It was best for him to leave. I told him my decision and assumed he would move out. Christmas and New Year's passed and he was still there. He didn't leave the house until January 21, 2008. The move was painful because he didn't have many friends, which meant I had to ignore my emotions and help him move to a friend's house. I later learned he was there for a couple of weeks then moved to a different place with his girlfriend, who was also married.

"I found out she was married fifteen days after I received Dean's email, when Dean's mistress's husband called and confirmed the affair. He felt I should know."

I shifted in my seat, not knowing how to respond to this hard-to-believe news.

"I staggered at the truth of the man's words," she said. "How could this happen? I'd seen signs but hadn't wanted to believe them. My beautiful, longed-for future crashed around my feet."

I sat pondering how many unfaithful husbands and wives had caused this kind of pain in their spouses. Now Carmen had become a statistic. Her husband's adultery brought her dream of a happy family to an irreparable end.

"Dean agreed to file for divorce. Of course, he took his time, as his new girlfriend also filed for divorce, and they used the same attorney.

"He ended up paying me child support of $619 monthly. He kept his own credit cards. I kept one of the cars and our home. My divorce became final."

Only the grace of God enabled Carmen to face the loss of her dream.

A Continuing Battle

Carmen said, "It's possible to find a smooth, mutual agreement between parents when a child is involved. However, because of the bitterness we both felt, my divorce turned into a nightmare. Michael became the victim, because his relationship with the two of us had changed forever.

"Later, Dean filed an affidavit with the court, stating his earnings were now less than mine and requesting more visitation time with Michael, which would reduce the amount of child support he owed. Because of his lower income, the court ordered me to pay him $306 a month. That decision represented a loss of $925 for me, since I no longer received the original $619 in child support. Anger rose up inside me.

"My ex-husband's betrayal and rejection increased when I realized he could freely move on with his new life without a financial commitment to us, while I was solely responsible for Michael's financial needs."

A New Plan

Carmen's ordeal caused her to think more seriously about her future as a single mother with sole responsibility for her son.

"I needed to generate additional money to cover the monthly payment to my ex-husband and also provide financial security for Michael's future and mine.

"God placed a desire in my heart to start undergraduate studies. Honestly, I thought it was a crazy idea. But God kept pushing me forward and opening the door for me to complete my schooling. I listened to His whispers and allowed Him to lead me. I thought I would fail, but God kept showing me how precious I was in His eyes."

I was grateful Carmen had let God's love fill her.

"After taking two classes, I fully embraced this as God's plan. He led me to take my time with my studies. I worked more than forty hours during the week and went to class three nights a week.

"My opportunity to work and go to school showed my son that even after a negative situation, positive things can happen."

"Carmen, you are an amazing woman full of abilities, and you're a wonderful mother."

Becoming Strong

"I'm grateful for the love Michael and I share. And God's love prevented my devastating circumstances from defeating me, as they normally would. My hard times produced greater personal development and spiritual growth. I felt more confident to handle my circumstances without relying on others. I knew God was with me.

"Even though I promised myself I would shield my son from my difficulties, he sensed my struggle to survive. He knew I couldn't provide for him as I had before, but he never complained.

"Many times, I had to borrow from one credit card to pay another. Other times, my cash flow was insufficient to buy groceries plus pay my child's basketball fees and purchase his uniforms. I took advantage of a payment plan with the basketball team. I shopped for specials and worked overtime when I needed groceries or money for his lunch account."

Carmen's willingness to try any option had pulled her through.

"My son's dad completely stopped helping with any expenses when he no longer had to send child support. He was an upset and angry man. My struggle was real, and not only financially. I soon fell behind in my child support to Dean, and he bullied me. I wondered when this ordeal would stop."

Friendship with God

"Amazingly, my turmoil and trauma drew me closer to God and much closer to my son. That's the way He works."

I loved the way Carmen had expressed the changes. "I'm praising God for never leaving you alone, Carmen, and for your closer relationship with Him and your wonderful son."

"God has been with me all the time. He helped me finish my MBA while going through the crisis of my divorce. When my mother was diagnosed with Alzheimer's and my sisters said they couldn't help her, I moved my mom into my home. God supported me physically and emotionally in the trauma of fully caring for her.

"God also gave me the wisdom and guidance I needed to take care of my teenage son alone. I still struggled because of the lack of financial help from Michael's father, but God placed a new job in front of me. I was already working as a paralegal, but another title insurance company offered me a paralegal job at a higher salary. I still work for that company."

Then Carmen recalled a special leading from God. "In the midst of all the confusion, I experienced one magnificent revelation from God. I still remember the morning I got up and told Him, 'Just as You give something to me, You can take it from me.'

"In that moment, I promised to trust in God and fully allow Him to guide my present and future finances. That became my first action toward releasing myself into the Lord's care. I finally understood that He provides, whether much or little. My part is to trust Him."

The challenges that would come to Carmen in the near future would help her see a brighter light from God.

"One Christmas, Michael wanted an Xbox. That year, I had no money for presents, and I had to explain that to my son. He understood, but I knew he was disappointed.

"Seven months before, I had started a new job. I went to work with a heavy heart on Christmas Eve. That day, the president of the company came to my office and closed the door.

"My heart stopped. I was sure they were going to let me go. But, to my surprise, the president handed me an envelope with a Christmas bonus inside. When he left my office, I knelt on the carpet and said, 'Thank You, God. I know this is Your work.'"

God must have been pleased that Carmen recognized all of this as coming from Him.

"After I left work that day, I drove to an electronics store and selected an Xbox for Michael. After the clerk rang up my purchase, I reached into my bonus envelope and paid cash for my son's longed-for gift, which was another miracle from God.

"That year was one of the happiest Christmases we'd ever had. Not only because of the bonus that allowed me to purchase Michael's gift, but also because I knew God understood my situation and was teaching me to trust Him in a new way."

When we see how much God knows and understands us, we are able to trust Him more. "That's such a beautiful story, Carmen. I can't even imagine the expression on Michael's face when he opened his Christmas gift."

"I loved watching Michael respond to my answered prayer. At that moment, I felt so loved by God."

A New Life

"Confronting these challenging issues gave me courage to let go of my fear of rejection and become the real person I am. My new freedom lets me live in stark contrast to my many years of bondage. From a young age, I saw my life as a jigsaw puzzle and thought my job was to place every single piece in the right place so my life could be perfect. When I discovered my ex-husband's infidelity, my puzzle crumbled.

"The many unsettling events in my life, like this one, led me to choose a new life of freedom, and live in the truth of God's Word."

She then shared two of her favorite passages:

> You will show me the way of life, granting me the joy of your presence and the pleasures of living with you forever. (Psalm 16:11)

> A final word: Be strong in the Lord and in his mighty power. (Ephesians 6:10)

"I no longer search for a picture-perfect life or expect perfection from the people around me. I've stopped judging others, because who am I to judge?

"Now I try to look at them with the eyes of my heart, realizing everyone contributes something special and unique. Life becomes more enjoyable when we accept one another as we are."

I wanted Carmen to see herself the way I do. "You're an accepting person. You bring joy to others through the joy you experience with your Father. I'm proud of you and the woman you've become."

"Thank you, Gail. The heavy stress I placed on myself for many years melted away when I surrendered every area of my life to God and allowed Him to lead me to His path of freedom."

Carmen and I are well acquainted with God's way of stepping in whenever the fear of rejection tries to defeat us. She told me how God had used a cashier in one of her favorite stores to remind her of God's protection.

Carmen had had a particularly stressful day, and evidently, it showed on her face. The cashier looked at her and said, "Please pray Psalm 91."

Ever since that day, Carmen prays Psalm 91 daily. Eventually she personalized verses 14–16 in this way because it made her feel close to the Lord:

> Because she loves me, says the Lord, I will rescue Carmen; I will protect her, for she acknowledges my name. She will call on me, and I will answer her; I will be with her in trouble, I will deliver her and honor her. With long life I will satisfy her and show her my salvation.

God protected Carmen from the effects of her father's early abandonment and her disintegrating marriage. He prevented her from pursuing goals that would have kept her in captivity. He gave her courage to face overwhelming adjustments in her life in the US.

Living on the Path of Freedom

The Lord also planned for Carmen to tell her story in this book. When I had space for two more chapters, I posted on my Facebook page: "Do you want me to share your story in my upcoming book, *Living on the Path of Freedom: Leaving the Fear of Rejection Behind?* Send me a brief overview of your story for me to consider."

Carmen immediately responded. After scanning the overview of her life, I confirmed to her, "I've chosen your story."

Later she told me, "Writing this story and being truthful with myself has helped me give each chapter of my life to God so I can continue seeing and experiencing my Father's light and love. I would like people to see that nothing is impossible with God. As long as we trust in Him and His timing, we can move mountains. We merely need to focus on Him and not our circumstances. Matthew 17:20 is one of my favorite verses."

> You don't have enough faith, Jesus told [His disciples]. I tell you the truth, if you had faith even as small as a mustard seed, you could say to this mountain, "Move from here to there," and it would move. Nothing would be impossible. (Matthew 17:20)

The day I confirmed that her story would be included, Carmen texted me. "I'm in tears. If I can give hope to one person through my story in your book, I know I will have contributed to God's work."

Are you perhaps the one who needs the hope Carmen offers today?

My Personal Prayer:

_____

_____

_____

_____

_____

_____

_____

_____

_____

_____

Bible Memory Verse:

Jesus looked at them intently and said, "Humanly speaking, it is impossible. But with God everything is possible." (Matthew 19:26)

Chapter Challenge:

- Has anyone ever left you abandoned and alone? Do you remember how you felt? Consider what God or other special people in your life did to help you feel secure again. Share your thoughts with a friend and pray together. Thank God for His emotional and physical protection.

  _____

  _____

  _____

  _____

  _____

- Do you remember reading about Carmen not having enough money to buy her son a Christmas gift and how God miraculously provided? Has God ever provided what you needed just in time? Take a moment to thank Him for His faithfulness.

  _____

  _____

  _____

  _____

  _____

- Have you ever created a dream and watched it fall apart? Journal about your experience. Include details of how God restored you and how He perhaps gave you a new dream. Recommit to following His lead and aligning your life with His will. Then watch Him fulfill the dream He planned for you.

  _____

  _____

  _____

  _____

  _____

Chapter 9

Light in the Darkness
Rosalie Flynn

"*I*'ve finally found liberty and peace in the Lord."

Rosalie lived sixty years in bondage—from an early age into her senior years. To receive admiration and approval, she performed the way she thought others expected. She readily said yes to every new responsibility. Though stretched to her physical capacity, she viewed each open door as another opportunity to prove how efficient, conscientious, and indispensable she was.

The rope that bound Rosalie to that hectic lifestyle unraveled when she became seriously ill. After she'd suffered three months, God showed her that He allowed her misery so she would lay aside her nonstop, carefully orchestrated life of service for a season.

We became friends through my former church in Columbus, Ohio, where she was an active member. The church supported my ministry for many years, and Rosalie heard about me.

During one of my annual visits to Columbus from my home in Orlando, Rosalie approached me after the church service. "Gail, I know about your ministry, and I'd like to help support you."

Our brief conversation that day birthed a special friendship. Little did we know that our bond would take us on a journey that led to the unveiling of Rosalie's secret life story.

Prior to my 2018 fall visit to Columbus, when Rosalie and I planned to get together, I received an email that caught me off guard.

She began with her usual update: "I've started organizing the fundraising events for our church's ladies club. I get overwhelmed at times, but I love it."

She continued, "I'm also coping with an illness that involved emergency surgery and a follow-up surgery the next morning. I'm still recovering and resting a lot, but I know God isn't finished with me yet."

Each time I inquired about her health, Rosalie assured me our breakfast date was on. We decided on a golf course restaurant near the retirement center where Rosalie lives. After picking her up, I drove over a bridge and veered into an empty parking slot near the walkway leading to the restaurant and the first-hole green.

When I pulled open the large wooden door of the restaurant, we heard boisterous laughter from morning golfers. The calm, middle-aged woman, who seated us near a window and placed menus on our table, had obviously grown accustomed to the rowdy environment.

By the time she returned with her coffee pot, we had glanced through the menu and were ready with our order of omelets.

Afterward, I looked across the table at my sweet, petite friend with her trademark short-cropped red hair. "Rosalie, I'm so glad we're finally together again and you've regained your strength."

Her loving smile warmed my heart. "Thanks for your emails that filled up the time between our visits. I'm eager to know if you got your books printed before you came."

"Yes, and here's your signed copy."

Her eyes lit up as she read the title, *Will the Real Person Please Stand Up? Rising Above the Fear of Rejection.* "I can't wait to read this, Gail."

The Unveiling

Tears filled her eyes as she looked at me with a sad smile. "You know things weren't easy in my family."

I reached out and covered her hands with mine. "When you first learned the title of my book, you implied that you knew about fear of rejection. But I don't know anything about your childhood."

After a long pause, Rosalie began. "My earliest remembrance occurred when I was about four years old. Perhaps that experience caused my feelings of rejection and insecurity.

"I lived with my mother and grandmother in a Los Angeles suburb. My parents had separated, and my dad had visitation rights and was allowed to see me privately.

During one of his visits, we were alone together in our living room. Suddenly, he picked me up, carried me to his car, and sped off."

My heart froze. Inside I cried for my dear friend Rosalie. "You were only four years old. How horrifying for you."

She nodded, sudden weariness clouding her eyes. "He drove me to a tavern-grocery store and left me in the car while he went inside. A stranger came out with him, supposedly a friend of Dad's. The three of us went to the man's house. They brought me inside.

"My dad left me sitting on a hard bench pushed against the wall in that unfamiliar place. I didn't know if or when he would come back to the house. Deep fear spread through me. Right then, at that very early age, I felt abandoned. I didn't know the woman in that house or the children playing on the rug."

The fear of abandonment couldn't have been greater than she felt in that moment. "Rosalie, you must have missed your mother so much and wondered when you would see her again."

"I was too young to comprehend what was happening, but I remember feeling alone. The other children looked at me with questioning eyes, probably wanting me to join them on the living room floor. But I needed to stay on that bench where I felt safe in my own space."

I asked, "How long were you there? Did the children's mother feed you?"

"I'm not sure, but I don't remember being hungry. I don't remember what happened when nighttime came. Perhaps I slipped from the bench to the rug and went to sleep.

"As another day began, I sat frozen and silent on the bench, waiting for my dad, or anyone familiar, to come and get me. My only recollection of the children's mother talking to me is when she came into the living room on the second day and asked my phone number. I'm glad I remembered."

"Why do you think she waited so long?"

"As I look back on this traumatic time, it all seems strange. I have no idea why the woman waited so long to try to locate my family, or why my dad's friend didn't help. Perhaps they didn't know my dad's plan or how to reach him, and they kept thinking he would return to pick me up.

"I heard the woman call my mother. Before I knew it, Mother and Grandma were at the house, along with a policeman. Mother and Grandma rushed to me, crying, but they were happy I'd been found. They praised God and thanked Him out loud. My grandmother was a Pentecostal minister, and she and Mother were prayer warriors, so they'd undoubtedly been praying they could find me."

What an incredible answer to prayer. "Do you have other memories of that day?"

"They knelt down beside me and said, 'You were so good to remember your phone number. It's a miracle.' I was crying, but their hugs calmed my young heart and made me feel secure. I can still hear the sounds of their happiness.

"During the ride home, they both watched for my dad, in case he pursued us. To hide me, they had laid me on the car's floor and covered me with a blanket. The trauma made me fearful, but I knew my mother and grandmother would protect me.

"I don't recall what took place once we got home. I do remember my mom and grandma's protectiveness after the kidnapping. I sometimes wondered whether Dad came back."

Surely they all remained fearful. "Did your father apologize or ask for your forgiveness?"

"No. If he had, I would surely remember it. From my teen years onward, I had many conversations with my dad, but he never brought up what he'd done. Perhaps he buried it in his subconscious. I always wondered why he didn't ask my forgiveness, but he never talked much about what was on his mind."

"It's strange that your dad didn't take you to his own house."

"I'm not sure where he was staying, because he and my mother frequently separated for a time. He may have been staying at his friend's house when he kidnapped me, but I didn't see him the whole time I was there. Maybe he told his friend he'd taken me out of a bad living situation."

I stepped away from my chair to hug her. As I released her, I could hardly bear the sadness in her face. "Such a tragedy without answers."

"Yes, it is. It's been difficult throughout my life."

Just then, our server arrived with our fluffy bacon-and-cheese omelets and refilled our cups with steaming coffee. The well-timed delivery gave us a chance to pause for a moment, and I silently tried to absorb the unbelievable story Rosalie had shared.

Continuing Fear

Once we'd eaten a few bites, Rosalie continued. "After the kidnapping, my dad stayed in the background for a while. He came to the house from time to time, but I always felt uneasy around him. I recall him whipping me when I was seven. I didn't come straight home from school as I was supposed to, but I went to a little boy's house instead. Dad waited for me with a belt.

"While looking at my baby book years later, I noticed that Dad wasn't in any pictures of my birthday parties before I was six. I do remember happy memories of Dad at several later parties."

I was glad for some good memories. "How did he respond when he came to your parties?"

"I don't remember, but every time I saw him, I felt the same underlying fear I had during the kidnapping. My mom tried to protect me, but she couldn't erase my memories."

No mother could have soothed a child who had experienced what Rosalie had.

Breaking Point

"Rosalie, you mentioned your parents were separated at the time of the kidnapping. Tell me more about them."

"I assume Dad and Mother didn't have a smooth marriage. Perhaps that was because Mother knew the Lord, but Dad called himself an atheist.

"My grandmother was a strong Christian and kept advising my mother to leave him. Mom sometimes thought about taking us children and leaving, but she kept changing her mind. She admitted, 'Your dad always sweet-talked me into staying.'

"Although their marriage was rocky, they had two more children, Larry and Isaac. My dad still couldn't connect with us, but life went on."

Concerned about her lack of connection with her father, I asked, "Did your mom and dad continue separating from time to time and coming back together?"

"For a while. But everything changed when I was eleven years old. One day, I came home from school, and Dad was in the kitchen, cooking. I greeted him and went to my room.

"Soon after, my mother arrived home and came into my bedroom. She told me to pack my bags because my brothers and I were going with her to a women's shelter. Mom had found love letters addressed to my dad in his overnight bag. We learned that on his overnight runs with the Southern Pacific railroad, he'd found a girlfriend in every town.

"The shelter looked so bleak and dank, I wanted to run away. But we stayed with Mother in the shelter until she found a small rental house in Columbus. The four of us moved there. In 1955, my parents divorced."

This made things final, so I wondered if she had any further chance for connection. "Did you get to see your dad after your parents divorced?"

"From age thirteen to sixteen, I saw him occasionally, when we lived in the rental house in south Columbus. When I was sixteen, we moved to a duplex in north Columbus, and he visited there periodically.

"On one of his visits, he brought me a bicycle. I have happy memories of Dad teaching me how to ride. Later, when the bicycle needed repairs, I wrote him a letter, asking him to come and fix it. Eventually, he came, and I was out riding again."

A Mother's Influence

At least she'd built a few happy memories with her dad after all the trauma. "Rosalie, how was your relationship with your mom?"

"My mother and I were close, but she was strict. During my elementary school days and beyond, she trained me to be responsible and dependable. Mom also insisted I must be perfect. I devoted all my energy to living out these three traits. I believed I had to show my capabilities to my family and others constantly in order to gain their approval.

"Any progress I made to achieve their approval was purely through my own efforts. I continued striving for perfection and strict compliance to rules throughout my entire life."

I now understood her a lot better.

Rosalie continued, "During my last two years in high school, my mother made me work and earn money for my school expenses and clothes. She wanted me to develop a good work ethic.

"After her divorce, Mom had to get a job because she received no child support. She took my father to court for support and won, but after a couple of months, he stopped sending money. As a result, we had to live in a low-income rental house. In reality, it was a shack with an old oil-burning stove on the outside.

"Since Mom worked, she left me at home to take care of my younger brothers and the housework. I hardly had time to play. All this responsibility stole my childhood."

Rosalie had told me about a conversation she recently had with a close friend. When Rosalie said something about her childhood, her friend burst out, "Your childhood? What childhood?" Rosalie received her friend's comment as confirmation that her mother never allowed her brothers and her to be children.

"She kept my younger brother Isaac so busy, he rebelled and ran away briefly when he was ten years old. My other brother, Larry, resented Mom so much, he threatened her with a knife when he was twelve and told her he was now in control. His actions landed him in juvenile detention. When he was released, my aunt and uncle, who had a son the same age as Larry, took him in as a foster child to give him a father figure."

"During a conversation with Mom when I was older, she admitted she'd made a mistake by not giving us children time to play while we were growing up."

"Rosalie, she definitely controlled the three of you. I wonder if your father faced that same problem."

"He used to say she nagged him all the time. However, in spite of my mother's strictness, she left me a legacy: my faith in God and my assurance of salvation. When my dad and mom were together, he always persuaded her to stay home from church. As a result, she didn't live for the Lord. However, after the divorce, she went back to the Lord and started taking us to Sunday school and church."

"I'm glad you and your brothers had a chance to go to church and receive some spiritual grounding."

"I enjoyed getting to make some friends at church. It helped me feel as if I had a life apart from working at home.

"My mom also loved to pray for me and my brothers. Once I was on my own, our phone calls always ended the same way: Mom reminding me, 'If you want prayer, day or night, call me.' Mother passed into eternity sixteen years ago, and I still miss her fervent prayers."

In spite of the hardship of her childhood, God gave Rosalie a gift: prayer as a sweet connection with her mother.

"As I think about my mom and what I've heard about her younger years, I surmise that the root cause of my mother's need for us to be perfect stemmed from her own insecurities. I imagine she fought insecurity all her life. Now that I see her from a different perspective, I have forgiven her, and I genuinely look forward to being with her in God's kingdom."

After learning more about Rosalie's upbringing, I understood why she became a driven person, intent on doing things perfectly and meeting everyone's expectations—especially her mother's. I was also intrigued with the soft, compassionate woman she had become after all she had endured.

From Darkness to Light

The morning was almost over, but Rosalie seemed eager to share more. "I must have kept these feelings of abandonment and insecurity buried all my life, because I never gave my kidnapping much thought until you asked me to tell you about my life."

"I'm sorry you had to bear that trauma at such a young age, Rosalie. Understandably, your young mind buried the incident. But when you remembered the memory and told me about it, you allowed the emotions of your trauma to surface, which exposed them to God's light. And His light broke the hold of those emotions. From now on, you can remember the incident, but it won't have a hold on you."

She swiped a tear from her cheek. "I'm thankful that God helped those emotions to surface. Now I understand why I feel free in a way I never knew before."

Later, during one of our phone calls, Rosalie would tell me about another turning point that took place shortly after her return from our breakfast get-together. As she recalled things she had revealed to me about her life, she felt a heaviness came over her. When the heaviness diminished, she suddenly announced out loud, "I forgive you, Dad." In that moment, she felt release. Her dad never told her he loved her or showed his love in a tangible way, but her forgiveness set her free.

A New Beginning

I thought of another question for Rosalie. "What is your relationship like with your dad now that you're grown?"

"Dad dated several women after my parents' divorce, and he remarried when I was already an adult. After that, Dad and I began to connect more frequently. He lived in another city, about a hundred miles from my home with my second husband.

"My father and I talked by phone and visited when we could. I remember one phone call when I was about forty. At the end of our conversation, I said on impulse, 'I love you, Dad.' This caught him—and me—off guard.

"He was speechless at first, but he finally responded, 'I love you.' I had waited a long time to hear those words from Dad, and I still cherish them today.

"This brought us closer, and on the next visit, we greeted each other with hugs. I'd suffered a lot in our relationship when I was a child, but little by little, our new relationship overshadowed past events."

Even though her dad never spoke to her about the kidnapping and didn't resolve that traumatic incident, God enabled them to have a closer relationship than before.

"That sounds like a sweet reunion. In a similar way, my dad and I were able to rebuild our relationship. My parents divorced when I was thirteen. When he and my stepmother, Connie, married five years later, they opened their arms to me and encouraged my visits. That gave my dad and me time to get to know each other in a new way, and it let us use terms of endearment we both had missed saying to each other."

"I'm glad that happened to you, Gail. We both experienced a second chance to know our fathers better."

Unwise Decision

Rosalie and I looked around and realized that most of the most people were finishing their lunches and leaving for another round of golf. We strolled around inside the restaurant for a few minutes, stretching our legs. As we came back to our table, I asked our server whether we could stay at our table for a while longer. She responded, "No problem. Can I bring you some fresh cups of coffee?"

Rosalie picked up where she'd left off. "Earlier, I mentioned my second husband. He treated me like a queen, compared to my first husband, who was an alcoholic. I was young and naïve and believed he'd quit drinking if I married him.

"Don and I were married about three years. Throughout this time, he drank and physically abused me.

"Don worked for a construction company. When they sent him to a construction site at the naval base in San Diego, we decided that our toddler, Madeline, and I would go along. He had arranged for a long-term monthly rent with a local hotel, which he paid out of his salary. Don's friend Jim, also a civilian, was his construction partner at the site.

"One morning, I saw Don off to work, but he didn't come back at the usual time. In the past, he'd sometimes stayed away for a couple of days on a drunken binge, so I expected him to eventually show up. This time, though, there wasn't much food in the refrigerator.

"After Don had been gone several days, Jim, his construction partner, came to the motel. He told me Don was dating a Mexican girl across the border. He said he felt sorry for me and thought I should know.

"The news shocked me. Don said he'd always been faithful to me; now I knew he hadn't."

The news had startled me as well. "With Don gone, what did you do?"

"The motel office asked for the monthly rent, but I didn't have any money. I told Jim that my daughter, Madeline, and I had nowhere to go. He talked to his sister Annie, who invited us to stay with her, her husband, and their two children.

"I gratefully packed our few belongings, and we went with Don to Annie's house. For the days I was there, Annie kindly hired me to take care of her kids."

I'm always amazed with God's perfectly timed provisions.

"I delayed telling my family about my predicament, because I wanted to find my husband. Jim took me where he thought Don would be, but he'd disappeared. He said Don accused him of having an affair with me. An affair was the furthest from the truth. Jim was not married and expressed only kindness to me. He was always gentlemanly and spoke no suggestive words.

"Then came the last straw. While I was staying with Annie, my husband's girlfriend called me and demanded that I send my credit cards to her. I knew my mother couldn't help me financially, so I immediately phoned my dad and told him what had happened. He wired money for our bus ride back to Columbus."

"Rosalie, you told me your mother wanted to leave your dad but never had the courage. I'm glad you did."

From experience, Rosalie said, "Abused women often have a hard time leaving their husbands. Many of these women think they love their husbands, so they convince themselves that he'll change. The husbands apologize and persuade their wives to believe the abuse won't happen again. Other women don't leave because they have nowhere to go.

"Don abused me both physically and mentally, while I was pregnant and afterward. Perhaps people wonder why I didn't leave him in the early years, but I was blind to the truth. I didn't want to leave, because—believe it or not—I still loved him and prayed and hoped he would change. He had a tragic end. His drinking caused diabetes, which was a determining factor in his death."

A New Season

"When I returned to Columbus, Madeline and I stayed with my dad and his wife, Barbara, for three weeks. Ever since Dad remarried in 1960, he seemed more mellow. It was easier to talk with him adult to adult. Through our interactions, I got over my fear of him."

Finally, a wonderful opportunity for Rosalie to let go of her many years of fear.

"I'm thankful to know your deep-seated fear melted away through those conversations with your father."

"I'm grateful, too, because it helped me thoroughly enjoy that longer visit with my dad and Barbara. Afterward, Madeline and I went to stay with Mother. She still lived on a low income and received help from the state.

"Not long afterward, Don and I divorced. I've never told Madeline much about her father, since she is autistic and mentally disabled. This is a blessing in disguise. One of her therapists informed me that if she didn't have this disability, she might become an alcoholic, since she has his genes."

Rosalie had told me that Madeline lives in a nice facility, where her needs are met and visits are permitted any time. I admire her healthy perspective on her daughter.

I knew I would always remember this long and special date with Rosalie because she'd revealed so much about her life. Many details shocked me. Rosalie was surprised when many memories and experiences surfaced once she uncovered the truth of abuse in her early years as well as her adult life.

As I looked at her sweet face, I saw how God had used her pain of rejection and abuse to mold her into an incredibly compassionate woman with a heart to spread hope and joy to downcast women.

"Rosalie, thank you for being willing to relive your painful experiences so others will know your story."

"Thank you, Gail, for helping me work through these difficult areas of my life."

I sensed this was a good conclusion to our visit. "Would you like to walk and talk outside for a little while before we leave? The beautiful golf course and towering trees along its borders would give us a refreshing change of scenery."

She agreed.

Rosalie and I finally walked away from our table and stepped out into the sunshine. As we breathed in the scent of freshly cut grass, I'm sure we both felt our muscles relax after our intense, but God-filled, time together.

We walked in silence for a few minutes.

Then Rosalie said, "Gail, my story is all about the ways God rescued me. Even though my father kidnapped me as a four-year-old, God took away the fear of my father so I could forgive him and rebuild our relationship.

"God rescued me from hard feelings toward my mother. He showed me how to forgive her by focusing on her faithfulness to pray for me. Recently, my brother Isaac told me, 'Mother's prayers were fulfilled when she prayed for me. When my life was going in the wrong direction, I believe it was her prayers that brought me back to the right path. I will always remember our mother's faithfulness as a prayer warrior for her children.'

"God also rescued me from my first husband's abuse and led me to my loving, caring second husband. I will never stop thanking God for all He has done for me."

"He truly rescued you, Rosalie, and redeemed what the enemy had stolen from you over all those years. He brought you out of hiding, and now you're free."

Rosalie paused for a moment and drew a sheet of paper from her bag. She handed it to me and said, "Don't you think this quote is perfect for our journey of learning to be ourselves?"

I read Rosalie's handwriting:

> Gail, I'd like you to read this quote from Nathaniel Branden's book *The Power of Self-Esteem:* "Persons of high self-esteem are not driven to make themselves superior to others: they do not seek to prove their value by measuring themselves against a comparative standard. Their joy comes from being who they are, not in being better than someone else."

"I love this quote, Rosalie. I'll share it with others who are on the same journey."

A hint of sadness tinged our goodbye, as we knew we wouldn't meet again for a year. But as I drove away, I thanked God for uncovering significant memories for Rosalie.

Health and Hope

The next year, Rosalie had another health scare. In February her doctor diagnosed her with double pneumonia and the flu.

She emailed me:

> During my two-day hospital stay, I experienced God's presence and peace. I made the hard but right decision to resign as coordinator of my ladies' club and reduce my other volunteer responsibilities.
>
> Often I reread Isaiah 43:18–19, the passage you wrote in the front of my book: "Do not call to mind the former things, or consider things of the past. Behold, I am going to do something new, now it will spring up; will you not be aware of it? I will even make a roadway in the wilderness, rivers in the desert."
>
> Those verses promise me that God is doing a new thing in my life. It's my responsibility to be aware and expect and be excited about this "new thing," whatever it may be.

After her recovery, she emailed me this update:

> Recently, God showed me His promise and hope in the form of a beautiful rainbow. I took in its splendor from my seventh-floor balcony. Later, I drove by a road sign that said, "You are loved by God." Those words confirmed that I'm on the right path toward a new adventure.
>
> I thank God every day for my freedom to be my own true self. He created me for His own pleasure, and I'm practicing to be His "present."

A New Name

During our previous visit in Columbus, I told Rosalie about my experience of learning the "new name" God had for me personally. My journey of discovery began when I read *Namesake*, a workbook by Jessica LaGrone. The author explained that God promises to give us a new name, and she included suggestions for discovering that name.

After asking God, I learned that my new name from Him is Joy Giver, which relates to the meaning of my given name: the Father's joy.

Rosalie was particularly intrigued when she heard about my experience. After talking with God, she felt His new name for her was "Giver." However, after she helped two women at the retirement center who were in serious physical condition, she sensed the Holy Spirit expanding her name to "Life Giver."

A French Experience

In September 2021, after a two-year wait caused by the pandemic, Rosalie and I finally met again. When I picked her up at the front door of her complex, she said, "I've chosen a special place for us."

Indeed, it was special—a small French café tucked into a line of small shops. Colorful artwork on the walls and the aroma of fresh-baked bread greeted us as we entered the restaurant.

Our round boutique table was barely large enough for the vase of bright flowers, our mouthwatering Monte Cristo sandwiches and fruit, and our essential cups of coffee.

We reminisced over the many things we talked about while together at the golf course and caught up on the events of our lives since then.

Rosalie said, "I lived with intimidation and rejection all my life until I read your book. You opened my eyes to the truth of what God says about me. I'm resting and basking in His love and assurance. Now I can accept His love, and that's all I need in this world. It's wonderful to be free.

"Also, the chapter on welcoming imperfection showed me how to let go of my need to have a perfect life. I no longer perform and try to please people in order to prove my worth. Now I'm careful how I use my time and say yes only to the specific opportunities God assigns to me."

Pleasure filled my heart. "Rosalie, your life has changed and I'm happy for you. God set you free from trying to gain from others what God has already given you: love and acceptance."

At the end of our lunch, Rosalie reached for her embroidered bag and pulled out a decorated sheet of paper. "Gail, I want to read the blessing I wrote for you."

She began with endearing words about our friendship. Then she spoke words of affirmation as if God were saying them to me:

> You are a beautiful woman, even though sometimes you don't believe it. Your heart to help people makes a difference in their lives. You've chosen to follow Me and please Me with your life and your words. You are free now, and I will use you to set others free.

Tears spilled onto my cheeks. Rising emotions tightened my throat. I knew God had chosen to speak through this dear friend, whom He had entrusted to me.

"Rosalie, I can't express how much you blessed me today. I will always treasure the words God gave you to say to me."

"You have blessed me too," she said. "I will never be the same."

To record the memory of our French date, I motioned to our server and asked, "Could you please take our picture?"

When I looked at the result, I was astounded to see Rosalie's beaming face—proof of the freedom and peace she now lives because God became the light in her darkness.

> For you have rescued me from death; you have kept my feet from slipping. So now I can walk in your presence, O God, in your life-giving light. (Psalm 56:13)

Rosalie's most devastating memory as a four-year-old girl stayed buried in the past until God marvelously revealed it to Rosalie. When she spoke of it, the buried emotions surfaced. Once exposed to God's light, the memory no longer held the same power over her.

When she acknowledged what she'd experienced, especially in her early years, she began to heal of her father's rejection and abandonment. God's love and faithfulness overpowered her insecurity, showing her that she would never be alone again.

The enemy doesn't want us to experience freedom. His strategies for keeping us in bondage aren't new. He repeats the same words of discouragement and defeat every time, trying to convince us to believe his lies about who we are and who God is.

When we believe the enemy's lie that we need to hide and protect ourselves, he thinks he won the battle. The truth is, God already won. He has defeated the enemy. When we live in the truth of God's identity and His victory, we become part of that victory.

To equip us for battle, God gave us His spiritual armor, as explained in Ephesians 6:11–18. When we put on His armor and declare we belong to Christ, we are fully protected.

> Put on the full armor of God, so that you will be able to stand firm against the schemes of the devil. For our struggle is not against flesh and blood, but against the rulers, against the powers, against the world forces of this darkness, against the spiritual forces of wickedness in the heavenly places. Therefore, take up the full armor of God, so that you will be able to resist on the evil day, and having done everything, to stand firm. Stand firm therefore, having belted your waist with truth, and having put on the breastplate of righteousness, and having strapped on your feet the preparation of the gospel of peace; in addition to all, taking up the shield of faith with which you will be able to extinguish all the flaming arrows of the evil one. And take the helmet of salvation and the sword of the Spirit, which is the word of God.
>
> With every prayer and request, pray at all times in the Spirit, and with this in view, be alert with all perseverance and every request for all the saints. (Ephesians 6:11–18 NASB)

The moment we begin our personal relationship with Him, God fills us with His power. By relying on His power, we can stand firm against the enemy's attempts to defeat us and prevent us from finding freedom.

Rosalie explained her progress this way: "God continually reminds me He loves me and will never leave me. I'm learning to stand up to the evil one and tell him that I am worthy when feelings of unworthiness creep in. But I know the truth of who I am now, and I will keep walking in freedom with God."

While Rosalie kept trying to win the approval of others, she lived in bondage. In her new life of freedom and peace, she serves others without wanting anything in return.

Rosalie is a shining light wherever she goes. We too can shine in this dark world. If God's light is in us, His light will shine through us.

When we choose to live in freedom, we can experience the joy and beauty of His presence. And we will continually see His light leading the way on our path.

My Personal Prayer:

_____

_____

_____

_____

_____

_____

_____

_____

_____

_____

Bible Memory Verse:

You light a lamp for me. The LORD, my God, lights up my darkness. (Psalm 18:28)

Chapter Challenge:

- Has someone in your family intimidated, abused, or rejected you? If so, have you told anyone? If not, seek a Christian counselor or other professional to listen and help you understand and deal with your trauma. Ask their help in bringing buried memories to the surface so the Lord can set you free.

- Do you identify with Rosalie and her goal of perfection? Talk with a friend who knows your tendencies and pray together. Acknowledging your tendency to hide behind perfectionism can begin your process of letting go of bondage and experiencing freedom.

- In what ways do you want to be a light to others? Journal your ideas and think of a church, organization, or small group where you might find an opportunity to shine the light of Christ.

_____

_____

_____

_____

_____

_____

_____

_____

_____

Chapter 10

What I Didn't Expect
Jennifer Johnson

"As a young woman, I traveled joyfully to another country to serve as a missionary. I never expected to leave wounded after a married ministry leader pursued me," Jennifer said.

I never imagined I would hear a story like this from Jennifer. I'm grateful we decided to have a video call. When I saw her dark brown eyes fill with tears, I wished I were there with her.

She continued, "In my short missionary career, I was shocked to observe a pastor and another ministry leader involved in extramarital affairs. Now the opportunity to be another leader's 'other woman' came to me."

"My heart breaks to learn about your trauma, Jennifer."

She and I had not been in touch during the years she was in another country, since email communication didn't exist in those early days. Now that she and her husband had a stateside ministry assignment, we wanted to reconnect.

"I've written my full story, as much as I can recall, and I want to share it with you. I'm glad this writing is behind me. It was difficult to relive the situation involving the leader, but this must be the right time. The Lord uncovered many thoughts I want to share with others."

The Beginning

I settled back in my chair as Jennifer continued her story.

"Through an experience I had as a student a few years earlier, I learned about God's desire for holiness in relationships. I dated a married man for a few months. He was separated from his wife, but the Lord quickly showed me He was not pleased.

"I was a young believer then. My personal relationship with Christ filled me with deep joy. I was flattered by this older man's attention, but when we began a relationship, my joy disappeared.

"A couple of years before, I learned the crucial difference between religious activity and a relationship with Christ. Now I once again became religious, in a sickeningly sweet kind of way. I'll never forget the day a friend confronted me about my relationship. She waved a booklet about the Holy Spirit in front of me, asking, 'What about this, Jennifer?' It was from a series of booklets on Christian growth that I had introduced her to.

"I knew I was out of God's will. Right away, I broke off the relationship. Thankfully, when I repented, the Lord restored my fellowship with Him. I committed myself to obeying the Bible completely as God's Word from then on. But I was still recovering spiritually when I joined the ministry full time."

I offered, "God is a gentle God, full of grace, isn't He?"

"Yes, He certainly showered me with His grace and forgiveness. A year or so went by, and I grew in my faith and saw positive changes in the lives of the women I was teaching. I had told my leadership about my past relationship, but they knew I was on the right track again. We all thought I was ready to go overseas.

"Maybe I was, and yet . . . I wouldn't have realized it then, but I was vulnerable. I think now that my distant relationship with my father had left me emotionally needy.

"I knew my father loved me, but he must not have known how to connect deeply with me. As a result, since my teenage years, I'd looked for a boyfriend to fill that void in my heart."

Her story reminded me of my own sadness, because my kind and thoughtful parents didn't know how to love me the way my young heart needed. I wiped away a few tears.

"Jennifer, I experienced that same kind of desire as a teenager preparing to enter high school. My mother and father didn't know how to build an emotional, loving connection with my brother and me. The emptiness in my heart created a longing to find a boy who would make me feel loved."

"Jesus's love drew me to Him, Gail. He filled the emptiness in my heart with His love. When I came to know Him, He began the beautiful process of transforming my life to reflect His.

"Somehow, in spite of my experience in college and the unfaithful ministry leaders I had observed, I still was truly naïve when it came to romantic relationships. I can't recall anyone ever telling me what to do if a married believer showed interest in me. Maybe it was supposed to be obvious."

I added, "But it isn't obvious, is it? I don't think many parents tell their daughters how to protect themselves in relationships with men."

Jennifer agreed. "Even as a second-term missionary a few years later, I had a lot to learn."

"Tell me more about what happened during that time."

The Enticement

"I was in my late twenties and a few years into my second assignment when this leader approached me after a ministry event. He merely said, 'I'd like to go out and talk.' I assumed he wanted to talk about the ministry. It seemed odd to have that kind of meeting late in the evening, but I came prepared to take notes. To my surprise, he took me to a nicer restaurant than I had seen in that city.

"While we waited for our food, he told me, 'I'm very attracted to you, Jennifer.' I was stunned. I had trusted and respected him. Perhaps I'd talked too easily with him in the past, but I never dreamed he'd say anything like that.

"I'd never had a serious relationship, but I had dated some. That kind of remark seemed familiar yet surreal because he was such a respected leader—and married. I didn't know what to say. I was numb. I didn't encourage him but sat and listened to him. The rest of the evening is mostly a blur.

"Later, I didn't know what to do. Should I tell someone? Should I disrupt his broad ministry and destroy his seemingly happy family? I couldn't imagine doing that, so I kept quiet."

"What a heavy load to carry."

"It was. At the same time, though, I had to admit I was flattered by his attention. I was lonely. I wanted to get married. I knew I shouldn't even think about his interest, but part of me wanted to—even though I had no desire for a long-term relationship with him."

I pondered Jennifer's struggle and wondered how she handled conversations with him after that evening.

Then she said, "Over the next few weeks, he called me at home and talked to me in person at the office now and then. I don't remember what we talked about. The similarity to my relationship with the married man in college did not occur to me. I was still perplexed, unsure what to do because of the impact it would have on the ministry.

"Since no one on his board confronted him, he knew I hadn't told anyone about his pursuit. This obviously made him feel safe to continue talking flirtatiously with me. I enjoyed our conversations to some extent, but I was increasingly troubled by his attention and the secret I didn't feel I could share with anyone. Thankfully, he did not attempt anything physical."

I felt angry that the leader had approached my friend in the beginning, and had also left her with the pressure of keeping their relationship secret. My only consolation was hearing that the relationship had not turned physical.

Jennifer looked down for a moment. "I'm not sure how long things would have gone on, or how far he would have taken his interest in me.

But one day, I suddenly understood the seriousness of the situation I tolerated by spending any time at all with this man. While visiting a friend in another town, I was surprised to receive a phone call from him. In those days of only landlines, he had gone to great lengths to find out my friend's phone number. I found this annoying and childish."

The Intervention

"On that call, he began to compliment my body in ways he—and no one else—had done before. I did not want to hear those things from him. Finally, I became angry and discerning enough to say to this older, admired leader, 'This has to stop.'"

I was shocked he would speak that way to Jennifer, especially while she was at a friend's house. "I'm glad you finally had courage to end it."

"I am too. I told him, 'I have to tell someone about this situation.' Surprisingly, he suggested I talk to another couple we both knew well.

"I called those friends and went to see them in their home an hour's drive away. We wept together as I told them what had happened. They quickly invited me to stay with them and counseled me to leave their country soon.

"In the next few days, I packed my car and moved to their home, taking my work with me. It felt strange to flee my home in that way."

I tried to envision the real impact this sudden uprooting had on Jennifer. Not to mention her realization of her part in the drama. "How surreal that must have felt, as if you were living someone else's life."

"I knew I wasn't the kind of person who did things like this. My friends contacted the man and his wife, and they began counseling them. I never saw that man again. As far as I knew, no one else knew what had happened, and I continued to keep it a secret.

"I stayed with my friends for a couple of months. I finished my office work, and also had time to talk with the Lord and begin processing what had happened. After that time, I returned to my apartment in the city and finished packing my things. Soon I got on a plane, but with some new unwanted 'baggage.'

"Within a few weeks of my arrival in the US, I stepped into a new assignment and started over."

I breathed a sigh of relief. "I'm glad you had safe and trustworthy people in your life who could listen to your secret and help you take the necessary steps to leave."

"They were the best people possible to help me out of that dangerous situation. They were horrified, but they were also loving and proactive. I will always cherish them and their friendship."

Important Lesson

Jennifer continued, "While I stayed with them, God spoke to me strongly about holiness and the sanctity of the marriage relationship. Hebrews 13:4 tells us, 'Marriage is to be held in honor among all, and the marriage bed is to be undefiled; for God will judge the sexually immoral and adulterers.'

"God's desire for holiness in our relationships became such a major life lesson for me that I have never forgotten it. If I had traded holiness for guilty pleasure, I'd have regretted it the rest of my life.

"What a tragedy it would have been to cause irreparable pain to my parents and siblings as well as to his family. Not to mention disappointing my ministry partners and dear friends who trusted me to live honorably on the money they invested in my ministry. Worse, I would have brought disgrace to the name of Christ and nullified much of the previous good that I and the ministry leader had accomplished. What sorrow everyone involved would have experienced."

I clearly understood the picture Jennifer described of the destruction that could have come, had she chosen that path. It made my heart skip a beat.

"A verse uppermost in my mind in those months before I left the country was 2 Corinthians 6:3, in which Paul says we must give no reason for offense in anything, 'so that the ministry will not be discredited.' The Lord was so kind to prevent me from giving much offense to the cause of Christ."

True Love Wins Out

Jennifer then told me about a happy encounter.

"In God's timing—several months after leaving my foreign assignment—I met a godly single man during some ministry meetings. He was wise and fun to talk to. We both wanted to serve as career missionaries overseas, so we soon began spending a lot of time together.

"Though I was now wary of married men, I didn't have trouble trusting a single man, especially this one. Others who knew him well saw him as a man of integrity. I loved that he didn't play games with me. How liberating it was to look deeply into each other's eyes and share the things that mattered most to us. Our hearts knit together during our months of courtship. When he proposed on a sunny hillside the following spring, it didn't take me long to say yes. I wanted to be with him. We got married a few months later.

"In spite of my confidence in him, I spoke to him only vaguely of what had happened, although it was a huge, painful memory. He did not try to force me to talk about it. I didn't know how things were in the ministry I had left behind, and I still didn't want to disrupt it."

Her husband obviously loved her. I admired the fact that he listened and accepted what she was willing to say without demanding details.

"We had been married a few months when God created a divine appointment that would help me greatly. One of the top female leaders of our ministry visited our area. She knew the leader from my previous assignment, and I felt free to tell her what had happened with him.

"She informed me that I was only one in a line of women he had pursued. The others reacted the same way I had—by keeping quiet. Thankfully, his actions must have come into the open, perhaps because of my friends' role in confronting him. He had been released from the ministry.

"I told her my husband didn't know what had happened. She gave me this advice: 'No secrets!' It was a relief, although difficult, to share the complete story with my loved one. He quietly replied, 'We might never have met if this hadn't happened.' I was awed to see that God truly had worked everything together for my—and our—good."

Just then, Jennifer's tall husband meandered into their den and bent down to the computer screen to greet me.

The Way of Holiness

When he left, Jennifer said, "My husband's unconditional love has wrapped strong and faithful arms around me as I've worked through the feelings that crop up from time to time. Every investment we've made in our marriage has fortified both of us against the enemy's attacks. We share our deepest thoughts and temptations with each other while knowing the other will love and accept us. That has been truly freeing."

I silently praised God for giving her such a wonderful husband. "His love and commitment are gifts of protection from God."

"Yes. The Lord has certainly used my husband's love to help me to heal. The enemy cleverly used my vulnerability to pull me into two ungodly relationships. Now Bible study and prayer help me refute the enemy's lies when he tries to tempt or discourage me. I can take a stand for holiness because I now know who I am in Christ: a holy woman who wants to glorify the Lord above all.

"God has continued to heal the pain this wayward leader left in my soul. It's taken time, but I learned that most married men don't have an ulterior motive when they say a kind word to me.

"Now I can look them in the eye in a normal fashion instead of quickly looking away for fear of seeing something that shouldn't be there. The Lord is restoring the confidence I once had that I can trust godly married men as my brothers. I'm regaining my freedom to interact with them as friends."

Jennifer's confidence in Christ helped her overcome fear.

"Meeting with a counselor also helped me better understand the issues of my growing-up years. It's normal to be open to the attention of others if your father didn't express his love to you. I'm not as vulnerable as before."

"You've made so much progress in your recovery, Jennifer. It's great to see your smile and witness your restored joy."

"I'm glad my joy is obvious! Years later, another female ministry leader, who had learned about the situation, asked my forgiveness on behalf of the ministry for what happened. Her words ministered deeply to me, in spite of the time that had gone by."

I thought about the secret Jennifer had been forced to keep. Now new evidence of redemption had surfaced, not only through the forgiveness of one compassionate leader, but also an apology and request for forgiveness from an entire ministry.

Heart Burden for Others

"The redemption I received in those moments became part of my healing. After all these years, my heart still rises up in anguish when married believers say they have no problem spending time alone with a person of the opposite sex—riding to events alone in a car or just the two of them spending a lot of time together in meetings, for example. Some married believers are even insulted that others might suggest the foolhardiness of this.

"But 1 Thessalonians 5:22 explains that we must avoid even the appearance of evil. Why not refuse to put ourselves in a place of temptation? Why not take every precaution to protect our families, our future, and our witness for Christ?"

I saw Jennifer's wisdom born out of her own experience. "Excellent questions for us to ask ourselves. That verse provides very clear guidelines."

"Attractions obviously happen, and unwise relationships are formed. They can happen to any of us," Jennifer said. "We need to remember that a malicious enemy plots our downfall and the destruction of our ministry. Should we give in to his plans? Of course not! We need to be on the alert.

"From my earliest days of following Jesus, the enemy tried to destroy my testimony, attacking me in my most vulnerable area. I praise God for protecting me and showing me how to fight those battles."

Words of Wisdom

Once again, I saw the power of the enemy. He's subtle, always looking for that crack through which he can pull us onto the wrong path.

"Jennifer, I'm grateful God brought you out of that devastating situation and into victory. He has obviously given you a burden to warn others."

"Yes, I hope others can learn from my story and be forewarned. It's wonderful to live without secrets."

A brief frown flashed across her face, before more words of wisdom came. "If I could talk with my younger self, I would say: 'Be on guard against the schemes of the enemy. Be especially careful in areas where your heart is vulnerable. If you find yourself in a compromising situation, don't hesitate to ask a godly confidant for help. Seek the Lord Jesus's love and friendship above all, and your joy and wisdom will deepen over the years.'"

A New Life

"I have experienced Jesus's promise in John 8:31–32: 'If you continue in My word, then you are truly My disciples; and you will know the truth, and the truth will set you free.'"

"I see that as you continued to walk in His truth, God freed you from everything that entangled you."

"Yes! My husband and I have been blessed with a normal marriage, complete with plenty of ups and downs. We have five beautiful children and enjoyed ministry overseas together for many years.

"In spite of the painful lessons I had to learn, I've found extreme joy in the freedom that comes from obeying God's Word."

When Jennifer said she wanted to share her story with me, I had no idea of the depth of her trauma. Yet it has become a story of victory. "Jennifer, you're a wonderful, courageous woman. I'm confident that God will use your story to protect many women in the future."

"Thank you, Gail," she said with a deep sigh. "Telling my story has brought further healing."

Jennifer had experienced something neither she nor I would expect. But even in the midst of the tragedy, God came to rescue her.

"I praise the Lord that His truth set me free. He promises to lead us in the way of holiness when we place our hearts and lives in His faithful hands."

> But now you are free from the power of sin and have become slaves of God. Now you do those things that lead to holiness and result in eternal life. (Romans 6:22)

Jennifer walked into a devastating experience she didn't expect or want. Here she was, a young woman serving God overseas, but needy, lonely, and full of the desire to be married. She was vulnerable, and the enemy easily swayed her to make unwise decisions.

Because of her experience, Jennifer realizes that many women are ill-prepared to spot or resist danger. They don't know the enemy always looks for ways to entice them to walk on the wrong path. He's subtle, so we must learn to identify his schemes.

The turning point came for Jennifer when God opened her eyes and she saw the truth of her ungodly decisions. God gave her strength to walk away from the wrong path and focus on Him again.

> Let's rid ourselves of every obstacle and the sin which so easily entangles us, and let's run with endurance the race that is set before us, looking only at Jesus, the originator and perfecter of the faith. (Hebrews 12:1–2 NASB)

Sin entangles us, trips us up, pulls us down, blocks our way, and delays us from running the race of life God set in front of us. That's why He emphasizes the reality of sin while promising forgiveness when we repent.

For everyone has sinned; we all fall short of God's glorious standard. (Romans 3:23)

Do not let sin control the way you live; do not give in to sinful desires. Do not let any part of your body become an instrument of evil to serve sin. Instead, give yourselves completely to God, for you were dead, but now you have new life. So use your whole body as an instrument to do what is right for the glory of God. (Romans 6:12–13)

If we confess our sins, He is faithful and righteous to forgive us our sins and to cleanse us from all unrighteousness. (1 John 1:9 NASB 1995)

But God showed His great love for us by sending Christ to die for us while we were still sinners. (Romans 5:8)

As you consider the sin you may have chosen, remember that Jesus died to save you from all your sin—past, present, and future. Tell Him you're sorry, accept His forgiveness, and willingly set out on His path again. Thank Him for His love, and ask Him to help you say no to sin so the unexpected won't catch you off guard.

My Personal Prayer:

_____

_____

_____

_____

_____

_____

_____

_____

_____

_____

Bible Memory Verse:

If we confess our sins, He is faithful and righteous to forgive us our sins and to cleanse us from all unrighteousness. (1 John 1:9 NASB 1995)

Chapter Challenge:

- Have you ever found yourself in a compromising situation, as Jennifer did? What decision did you make? If you chose not to follow God's way, tell Him what happened. Repent of your sin by telling God you're sorry and turning away from your sin. Ask Him to forgive you, then accept His promised forgiveness. He will help you to turn from your own ways and begin walking on His path again.

- If you know of a person who struggles with doubting whether God will forgive her for her sin, ask her to meet with you. Share your story with her, because hearing someone else's story of forgiveness often gives people hope. You may want to read the above verses to her. That way, she'll see God's willingness to forgive if she repents and asks for His forgiveness.

- If you have young children, grandchildren, nieces, or nephews, consider what advice you can share to help prepare them to make godly, healthy decisions when they form friendships with the opposite sex. Consult with friends who may have specific guidelines you can relay to these young people to protect them from making wrong decisions.

Chapter 11

A Heart of Gratitude
Lisa D'Aloise

"*I* thought John and I would grow old together."

With tears in my eyes, I hugged my new friend as we stood in Susan's living room prior to a small dinner get-together. After twenty-two years of marriage, Lisa lost her husband, John, to bladder cancer. She had been John's caregiver and watched him suffer.

Now a widow, Lisa wrestled with the grief and heartbreak of losing John only two months earlier, forcing her into an unexpected and unwanted season. Tonight would be her first time at a gathering without John. I prayed for God to strengthen her.

Lisa made it through dinner, though we all missed John and felt sad for Lisa. Being with friends and reminiscing about John seemed to soothe her heart.

I never dreamed Lisa would volunteer to tell me her life story years later.

We chose Wednesday for an interview at her home. That morning, I wound my way from south Orlando to the smaller, pleasant city of Oviedo.

As I turned the last corner, I spotted her beautiful, taupe-painted, two-story home and pulled into the driveway. I sat in my car for a moment, praying for courage for Lisa to share her sad story and tell me how God helped her walk forward.

As soon as I rang the bell in the wide alcove, the door swung open. "Come in," Lisa said. She led me through her lovely living room with its welcoming beige and burgundy decor.

As we neared the kitchen, she turned and asked, "Do you want to sit outside?"

"I'd love that, Lisa." As we stepped outside to her large patio, I said, "How beautiful and peaceful."

I noticed the expansive tiled floor and large gray-smoked glass table and chairs, but my gaze quickly swung to the glistening aqua water of the adjacent large pool. The cheery sunshine and unclouded blue sky created the perfect setting for our personal soul-searching interaction.

Lisa handed me a glass of cold water, and we settled into padded wrought-iron patio chairs.

As I pulled out my lined pad to capture details, I heard Lisa say, "You want to know my fear-of-rejection story?"

Lisa's question caught me off guard. I clarified, "That's the underlying theme, but I want to know about your childhood, family life, married life, and any significant adult discoveries you've made."

Growing-Up Days

"I'm the younger of two daughters. Linda is two years older. I had an absentee father," she said. "He came home from work at GE every day at five thirty, expecting Mom to have dinner ready. After the four of us ate, he always disappeared to the workshop he'd built in the basement for his TV repair side job. I don't think he needed the extra money. His choice to disengage with us left a void in my heart.

"My dad never expressed love to me or my sister. Determined not to make waves, I didn't talk to him much. I became a perfectionist and got all A's in school in an attempt to catch my father's attention."

I identified with Lisa's perfectionism. Many people choose this lifestyle if they lack love, admiration, and affirmation from someone they look up to.

"Whenever a girl told me her dad called her 'princess,' or 'daddy's little girl,' I felt like crying. I never was daddy's little girl, but I thought that must be awesome.

"Instead of receiving love and attention from my dad, I endured his verbal abuse and frequent silent treatments. Looking back, I realize my mom wasn't aware of the impact my dad's behavior had on me. She simply made excuses for him and thought things would get better. She often said, 'Don't upset your father,' or 'Don't let your father see you cry.' As a teenager, I wanted to stand up to his abuse and silence. But I wasn't brave enough."

Silent treatments are cruel enough. But since he also abused her verbally, I understood why she couldn't stand up to him.

"When I was small, Dad made it known that he had wanted me to be a boy. He dreamed of playing sports and hunting with his son. I convinced myself he was disappointed in me. I tried to make up for being a girl by playing sports as a teenager."

"It's so sad that you didn't receive the love you needed from your father, Lisa. It wasn't your fault you were born a girl."

"Right. My sister often got in trouble because she was bold, sometimes calling my dad out. Once Dad whopped Linda on the side of the face. Her ear started bleeding because the force had ripped out her small pierced earring."

Lisa continued. "My only lifeline of love was my grandmother on my mother's side. Our family lived in Buffalo, and she did too. I got to visit her a lot. Grandma was loving and caring. During my visits, I got lots of hugs. I drank in her affection, and I loved to bake with her. She was a Christian, so we also went to church together. But she and Grandpa moved to Leesburg, Florida, in 1972, when I was seven years old. After that, we saw them only twice a year."

"My grandmother was my lifeline too, Lisa. I have many memories of helping in her kitchen, drinking her homemade lemonade, and playing in her backyard. Receiving our grandmothers' love helped to fill our empty hearts when we both felt unloved in our immediate families."

"My dad's parents also lived in Buffalo. I especially enjoyed my grandfather. He had a stroke when I was only four years old, but I remember people saying he used to be the life of the party. Later, as a young mother, I drove up north to show my six-month-old son, Sean, to my family.

"As soon as my grandfather saw me walk in with Sean in my arms, he beamed. He couldn't speak, but even without an introduction, he knew this was his grandson. Watching my precious grandfather cradle my son with love in his eyes has become my favorite memory of him."

Just then I caught movement out of the corner of my eye. Looking toward the pool, I saw Lisa's multicolored cat skirting the edge of the pool. Focused on his mission, her cat hurried around the corner toward the patio door. Seconds later, with ease, he leaped through the cat door, positioned in a low side window of the kitchen.

I turned to Lisa. "That made my day. You know I was looking forward to meeting the famous Dash. He's a beautiful cat. I should have expected he wouldn't give me the time of day."

That brought laughter from Lisa. "He's not sociable around other people, but he snuggles with me every night. God gave me the perfect cat."

Result of Rejection

"I believe my lack of relationship with my dad fostered my fear of rejection and abandonment. It made me look for love in other places. My main purpose of dating as a teen was to gain love and attention from a guy.

"I had a few boyfriends in high school. When I was eighteen, I got to know blond-haired, blue-eyed Brian. We were in the same group of friends. Brian was nineteen and planned to attend a local college in Buffalo. His girlfriend, Victoria, who was also in our group, planned to go as well.

"Brian and I began spending time together, but we hid it from Victoria. Early in our relationship, he asked me to come to his mom's house, where he lived. That night I slept with him, and other nights as well.

"I didn't know what I was doing. Getting away from my father was my driving force, and I liked Brian's attention."

I asked Lisa, "Weren't you concerned about Brian's mother?"

"She knew about me and didn't care what happened upstairs. Apparently, his mother did her own thing, and he did his. Both parents were alcoholics. They were already divorced when I met Brian. He and his younger brother, Joe, lived at his mom's house.

"Alcohol was his mom's life, but she was a high-functioning alcoholic with a responsible sales job. I saw Brian starting to follow in his parents' footsteps. His drinking patterns and his unstable homelife should have warned me about him. But my search for love blinded my eyes."

I winced, knowing what was probably ahead.

"Brian enrolled in college, and I registered the following year. He had broken up with Victoria by then. However, he wasn't good at totally closing out relationships. He held on to his relationship with her, while he and I continued to see each other.

"After he cut Victoria completely out of his life, Brian and I immediately began a serious relationship."

Hopes Dashed

"In 1984, Brian's mother wanted to move to Florida and asked us to come too. We both dropped out of college and left with her."

"What was life like for you, living with Brian and his mom?"

"Brian's mom continued to drink, and her life became chaotic and unpredictable. She blamed us for random things, like money missing from her purse, although she'd spent it while she was drunk. Brian and I had a car accident that was not our fault, but when she found out, she believed it was our fault. Brian's father knew what she was like and gave Brian money for an apartment, so he could get away from her. We moved out, and Brian severed his relationship with his mom.

"I moved into Brian's apartment, and we got married two years later. We both wanted a child, so several years later, we planned to start our family. When I became pregnant with Sean, I couldn't wait to become a mother. My only sadness was that my dad would never see his grandson. He died before I became pregnant."

"That's a sadness that would never go away. Perhaps you could at least anticipate happy things ahead for you and Brian."

"I would have, but soon after I got pregnant, the responsibility of fatherhood became real to Brian. That thought lay heavily on his mind, so he started drinking more, trying to deal with his anxiety. This should have been a wake-up call for me, but I tried to ignore it."

Wake-up calls can be easily missed when we picture joy in front of us.

"I drank some in college but not as much Brian. I knew we both needed to grow up and quit partying. Brian realized he needed to change his ways, especially his drinking, but he didn't seem to try. The anticipation of becoming a mother made me happy. The thought of fatherhood still overwhelmed him.

"By the time Sean was born, Brian was drinking heavily, which made me angry. I was a store manager for Eckerd Drugs and was trying to raise our child. Brian worked in apartment maintenance. We argued constantly. He was mad that I was mad, and that became a vicious cycle."

I felt sad about Lisa's heartache and disappointment during a time that should have been happy.

"Our family in Buffalo wanted to see the baby, so I decided to take him there for a few days. My mom and grandmother were delighted to see six-month-old Sean. I also visited Brian's brother and father.

"On my last evening in Buffalo, Mom handed me a soft baby blanket. 'Your dad purchased this for his first grandbaby.' My heart melted. She also said something else, which I will cherish forever: 'One of the last things your dad said was that he wished he'd been a better father.'

Knowing my dad felt that way in the end helped my healing. At age twenty-five, I could finally forgive him for his verbal abuse and for withholding love from me."

My heart filled with thanks to God for giving her this inside glimpse of her father. "How sweet to see those signs of love after all you'd been through with your dad."

"As special as that was, it didn't prepare me for what waited for me back in Florida. After I came home, Brian said he wanted to go to rehab. I wanted to see him get sober, so I agreed with his plan.

"Two days later, he entered a thirty-day program. I hoped it would make a difference. By then, he'd had pancreatitis several times. He wasn't doing well, physically or mentally. According to protocol, the first seven days of rehab are considered a family-blackout period, so we had no communication.

"During that blackout time, a neighbor approached me and said, 'You should have seen everything that went on while you were gone. Brian and one of our neighbors had a good time together.' Ironically, she saw the woman nearby and said, 'That's the one.'

"I glanced over at the woman, and reality set in."

I tried to shut out the vision of this scene, but I couldn't. I had a feeling I knew exactly what she would tell me next.

"I'd had some notifications for unusual credit card expenditures while I was gone. Now I had an explanation, but I couldn't talk with Brian yet because he was gone."

My heart sank. Here was Lisa, trying to be a good mother to her son, but Brian cared only about himself. "That was another shocking heartbreak for you, Lisa."

"Yes, I could hardly take it in." She paused, her gaze drifting toward the pool. "Apparently, the girlfriend didn't know about Brian's rehab, because she kept calling our apartment. Every time I answered, she hung up. Each phone call deepened my anger.

"When seven days had passed, and I finally had a chance to talk with Brian, my first words were, 'Tell your girlfriend to quit calling the apartment.' I wanted him to know I knew what was going on. All he could muster was a weak, 'Okay.'"

That didn't sound like remorse to me.

"During the month Brian was in rehab, I was physically sick. I couldn't sleep, and I saw a psychiatrist for antidepressants. When I went in for a follow-up appointment, I informed her that the pills weren't working. She asked whether I was sleeping and eating. When I told her yes, she said, 'Then they're working.' I wanted more. I wanted a happy pill.

"Family counseling is required during rehab. Brian and I had to talk about our situation with the counselor—and everyone else in the circle. Each person had to share. At the end of the first session, a woman said to me, 'All is not lost, Lisa. You can mend your marriage.' I strongly doubted that possibility."

"How were things after Brian finished with rehab?"

"Once he came home, our fighting resumed. Neither of us wanted to change. We both continued with our dysfunctional, codependent relationship."

Hesitating, but wanting to know, I finally asked Lisa, "Did you and Brian talk about his unfaithfulness? What did you say to each other? Did he give any indication that the affair was over?"

"I don't remember a lot of the conversations about his infidelity. I think it was just a fling fueled by alcohol. This was Brian's first time to hit rock bottom, and that probably prompted his decision to go into rehab. Looking back, I realize he had to be filled with guilt and shame."

"Did you see changes in his drinking after rehab?"

"I did at first. But he soon started drinking again. My desperation made me remove my rose-colored glasses, and I saw everything clearly for the first time. Brian was drinking heavily and seemed unwilling or unable to stop."

Downhill Plan

"I didn't want Sean to grow up in the middle of our fights. I naïvely thought things might get better if we moved up north, with different scenery and with family members around us. Plus, this would get Brian away from his drinking buddies and the other woman. Honestly, I also wanted to go home in case things didn't work out between us. I was still quite angry.

"We moved back to Buffalo and rented an apartment. But his drinking and our fighting continued, and I realized I couldn't live that way anymore. The reality caught up with me: Brian would never change.

"It all came to a head early one morning. I was downstairs getting ready to fix breakfast when I remembered a recent fight. Brian had yelled at me, 'Why don't you just leave?'

"While I tried to push that memory away, Brian came into the kitchen. He asked an innocent question: 'What are you doing today?' Something snapped in me. I looked at him and said, 'I'm doing what you asked me to do. I'm leaving.'"

I was shocked about their conversation, but I agreed that Lisa needed to take a step forward.

"Eyes wide, Brian watched me grab Sean. I marched up to our bedroom, packed two suitcases, and brought them downstairs. Then I went back for the baby. When I brought Sean downstairs, I found Brian sitting at the breakfast table. I gave him no chance to ask about Sean. I simply put the baby and the suitcases in the car, got in the driver's seat, and drove across town to live with Mom.

"Since I couldn't find a way to live with the fighting and deal with the truth of Brian's infidelity, I had to leave. Still wrestling in my mind that evening, I looked in my Bible to see if it was acceptable to separate from him. I found a verse that said a man could leave his wife if she was unfaithful. I decided that must apply to the wife as well.

"Brian and I had dated for four years and been married for six. We officially divorced when Sean was two years old, but our marriage had ended in the year before. We agreed on shared custody of Sean, with visitation for Brian every other weekend."

"Did Brian pay child support?"

Lisa hesitated. "Child support is a long story. He paid off and on. I had to garnish his wages, but he did pay his arrears in full after Sean was eighteen. As far as visitation goes, Brian continued to drink, was in rehab several other times, and still suffered from pancreatitis attacks, so his visits were unpredictable. Meanwhile, I did the best I could to make Sean happy.

"One year, when Sean was nine, he spent Christmas with his dad—in the hospital. Brian had another pancreatitis attack, and he took our son to the hospital with him instead of calling me to pick him up. I learned about this later and was furious."

Blessed Security

"My mom already knew that Brian and I fought a lot while we were married. She also knew he'd been to rehab. Living with Mom gave me a sense of safety and peace again. I began to regain my strength, along with hope for a future. One day she said, 'It's such a blessing to have you and Sean here with me.' I needed to hear that."

"I'm thankful you had your mom to turn to."

"She's always been there for me."

That gave us something to smile about. "Lisa, thank you for telling me about this sad part of your life. Do you want to take a break?"

She readily agreed. When I returned to the patio, I saw that Lisa had set a refreshing glass of iced tea by my place. As she wandered back, we stood side by side, gazing at the beautiful azure water rippling gently as the breeze blew over it. The beauty around me shoved the sad, devastating parts of Lisa's story into the background. I was ready to hear about happier times.

A Surprise Visitor

As we settled back at the table, I learned that Lisa met John shortly after her divorce. John walked into Phar-Mor, a large pharmacy in Niagara Falls, New York, where Lisa worked in retail management. As he approached her, she noticed his kind brown eyes.

John posed a serious question. "Where's the card aisle?"

Lisa merely smirked and pointed directly behind her.

Though unimpressed with John, Lisa still engaged in casual conversation whenever he wandered into the store. The variety of reasons became comical.

A few conversations later, John asked, "Do you want to catch lunch?"

"I can't leave the store that long," Lisa said, "but I could go for coffee."

They chose the Starbucks on the corner.

As a result of Brian's betrayal and her depression, Lisa weighed only eighty-seven pounds. She said, "I felt too sick to eat and often dipped into depression. However, I figured I could make it through the coffee break with John.

"On our mini-date, John confessed, 'The first day I met you at Phar-Mor, I was on a mission. I was checking out girls because I didn't want to be alone all summer.'

"I listened to John's saga," Lisa said, "but at that point, I hated men."

John's persistence paid off. She accepted a date with him one evening. There she learned that John had been married, but after discovering his wife was cheating on him, he filed for divorce. Their son, Johnny, lived with him, but Johnny's mother had visitation every other weekend.

It would take Lisa a little longer to tell John about Brian, and to regain the weight she had lost because of his betrayal.

"Once we were seeing each other frequently, I relaxed and became more willing to share the details of my first marriage. Before moving ahead, though, I went to the den and pulled a notebook from my desk drawer. I wanted to review the two criteria I'd written down for a potential husband. I turned to the page with my list."

She explained to me the conditions she had listed.

1. He must love his mother.
2. He must treat his mother well.

"I valued these criteria because I knew they would show how a man would treat me. While spending time with John and his parents, I observed their relationship. And I saw how he treated his mother. John received a top grade on my test."

Romance Arises

Since John passed Lisa's exam, I wondered where their relationship went from there.

"Soon after that," Lisa said, "John and I attended his brother's wedding. After the ceremony in the church sanctuary, we walked downstairs to the reception. Soon the music began to play, and John led me out onto the floor. While we danced, John said, 'We could do this.'"

His comment puzzled Lisa. "I looked at him and said, 'You told me you'd never marry again.'

"Gazing into my eyes, with obvious love, John simply said, 'Let's go shopping for rings.' Then he leaned forward and kissed me.

"My heart soared. I loved him, and I believed he and his whole family had accepted me. The warm atmosphere they created for me was a welcome change from my experiences in my own family."

I sighed with delight. "What a wonderful love story. God knew John was the man who could heal your heart."

"Yes, everything fell into place. John and I got married and settled into an apartment in Buffalo. Sean lived with us, and John's son was there every other weekend. Before our wedding, John said we were both in this a hundred percent, and that we will never consider divorce."

Lisa said, "John was Catholic when we married. I saw a generous heart and soul in him. We visited a couple other churches, and his view of God expanded. One day, God grabbed ahold of John. From then on, we grew together in our faith. We joined a church, volunteered, and got to know the church family.

"One thing I loved about John was the way he always built me up and believed the best of me. He was a real estate agent for RE/MAX in Buffalo. When I was laid off from my job, John said, 'You should go into real estate at my company.' I'd never thought about that profession, but I took the first step and applied for a job there. This started me on a journey I've loved all these years."

An Idea Blooms

It seemed a perfect fit with both of them working as real estate agents for the same company.

"Unexpectedly, John said to me one day, 'I think I'll get my Florida real estate license.' He had taken some courses in Florida, and some people in Buffalo told him how much better business was down there.

"John had great aspirations. He always moved quickly on each decision. Forgetting that fact, I told Mom that at some point John and I would eventually move to Florida. She responded, 'Eventually? You'll be there before you know it.'

"She was right. John and I soon moved here to Oviedo, Florida, where we enjoyed our new home and our work in real estate."

"John's news of a move was shocking at first, but it turned out well, didn't it?"

"It definitely did. My mom took care of both my grandmothers in Buffalo, but when they passed away, she moved here too. I enjoyed having my mom nearby, and she would be a great support when John got sick."

Unexpected Future

"John and I planned to buy a condo at Cocoa Beach and become part of a church family there when we retired. We both looked forward to 'growing old together.'"

The sweet expression on Lisa's face about this happy memory shifted quickly as sadness descended. "In January 2015, while John and I enjoyed a weekend out of town, he developed a blood clot in his urine.

Immediately upon our return to Oviedo, John saw his primary-care doctor. The blood tests showed cancer. He began holistic supplements to strengthen his immune system and fight the cancer.

"In May 2016, after many doctor visits and no change in the tumor, John had his bladder removed to decrease the potential spread of the cancer. The blood tests and scans indicated the cancer was contained in his bladder. However, surgery confirmed the cancer had spread to other organs."

The kind of report every cancer patient and family member dreads receiving.

"I continued to hope for a miracle. But I knew I needed to prepare to lose him. As John's illness progressed and the doctors could no longer help him, we brought in hospice. We moved a hospital bed into the living room, where friends could visit.

"After a courageous fight, John died on February 2, 2017. I knew the day would come, but I could hardly grasp the truth when it did. My mom and John's parents stayed with us while he was sick, but his parents left before he passed. They couldn't bear to watch him die.

"John's sister, Maryann, Sean, and I were at John's bedside when he passed. The three of us cared for him his last three weeks, and we have a bond unlike any other."

"The reality of loss is so difficult to bear. I'm grateful for the strength and encouragement God gave you, Lisa, throughout your sad journey."

"I couldn't have survived without God. One day while I was holding John's hand at his bedside, he looked at me with his beautiful brown eyes, smiled weakly, and said, 'Lisa, I love you so much. I don't want to leave you, but it seems this is God's will. You are a beautiful woman, and I want you to find a wonderful man who will love you as much as I do. Please be open to that.'

"I smiled at him, unable to hold back my tears. That was John, always thinking of me and not himself. Our last kiss was bittersweet."

I choked up as I pictured them together. "That's so touching, Lisa. Has knowing how much John loved you helped you on this new journey?"

"His love holds me up. Another day, near the end of his life, I was sitting with John, and he motioned for me to come in close to him. I expected a quick kiss. Instead, he whispered, 'Thank you for being my wife.' I'll never forget his words."

"Lisa, now that some years have passed, what are your plans for the future?"

"When John died, I couldn't imagine ever wanting anyone else in my life. Now, after five years without him, I know John would be happy if I met someone. I'm open to that possibility because of what John said to me."

New Opportunities

"I still get sad about John, but when I consider all the opportunities God gives me to help others, I'm grateful."

"Tell me more."

"After John died, I joined the hospice's Young Widows grief group for people under the age of sixty-five. I remained friends with them after our eight weeks of counseling together. The truths I learned during those weeks helped me grow stronger emotionally."

A Turning Point

"In 2021, I started seeing a counselor who is also a gifted prayer warrior. One of our sessions became a turning point for me. She observed that I focused on negative things in my life as a result of believing the lies Satan told me about myself."

As I pondered what Lisa's counselor had explained, I saw more clearly the connection between our negativity and believing Satan's lies about us. It can be subtle.

Lisa said, "As she prayed to God on my behalf, God gave her words to cast Satan from my life, in the name of Jesus. Then she asked God to show me truth.

"God answered that prayer. I heard these words from Him in my spirit: 'You are loved. I want to spend time with you. You are unique and special. I am holding you up.'"

I wiped away a tear as I sensed the intimacy of that moment.

"My counselor helped me understand that Satan listens to our words. He studies our behavior. He knows what we believe. He brings up issues we worry about. I realized I was in a vulnerable time in my life and was susceptible to Satan's words."

I listened closely. "My counselor told me that as believers, we're in an intense spiritual battle. We need to stand strong in our faith so the enemy doesn't think he's winning. I learned that when Satan tells me I am unworthy, I can ask God for words of truth and then say those words out loud to Satan.

"I continually pray and ask God to help me keep my mind on Him and put my belief and trust in Him. Hebrews 12:1–2 reminds me to 'run with endurance the race that is set before us, fixing our eyes on Jesus, the author and perfecter of faith.' I discovered that, by fixing my eyes on Jesus and staying available to God, I can live a purposeful life. My faith has grown. My relationship with God is deeper. I hear His voice more easily. I have a deep desire to put my whole heart into what God is calling me to do."

"What are some of those things?"

"I resumed leading the women's weekly Bible study group at my church. As we study the Word of God together, apply it in our lives, and share personal experiences each week, we get to know God and each other better.

"Also, I joined a team at my church that began making mission trips to the Dominican Republic, where an American couple from our church had a ministry. We made many trips to take personal supplies for the people and to help build and repair churches. Eventually, the women on our team planned a two-day spiritual conference for the DR women as a personal touch and to build their faith and vision. We also taught the local women a trade, such as jewelry making, so they could support their families. The sewing classes enabled many women to begin their own businesses.

"The far-reaching impact we had in these people's lives, both spiritually and economically, will always remain in my heart."

I could easily picture those women creating beautiful crafts, and the thrill Lisa experienced as she watched them.

"My latest burden is to help fight human trafficking," she said. "If God wants me to become involved in this cause, He'll show me."

Lisa had definitely become a woman with a God-given purpose. "Your ministry is inspiring. I've loved hearing how you're living out God's purpose."

The Role of Gratitude

"Recently, the Lord showed me that gratitude is one way I can stay centered on Him."

"Great reminder, Lisa."

I looked over at the glittering pool, a sense of peace washing over me. Somehow the fresh air, the colors of creation surrounding us, and Lisa's experiences of life after heartache blended into a picture of hope.

Lisa stood from her perch at the table. "Gail, follow me into the kitchen. I want to show you something."

As we stepped from the patio into her house, Lisa led me around the corner and pointed to a large black chalkboard. She said it had hung on her kitchen wall since she and John moved in years ago.

"After John passed," Lisa said, "my friend Susan and I created a new kind of blackboard together, one of our many projects to keep me busy. For many years, I wrote my grocery list on it. Now it has become my Gratitude Board, where I write one blessing every day. That makes all the difference in my perspective."

All of Lisa's friends, including me, wait to see what God will do in Lisa's life this year. One thing is certain. Lisa's long list of blessings—God, health, strength, Dash, family, friends, church, and many more—helps her rise above her circumstances and remain grateful to God every day.

Lisa's life did not unfold the way she'd dreamed. Abandoned by her father and betrayed by her husband, her heart had been crushed. Then, as she looked forward to her marriage to John, she envisioned a loving and accepting husband.

John was that kind of husband. Together they built a wonderful, Christ-centered life. As the years progressed, they enjoyed each season together. They looked forward to moving to Cocoa Beach when they retired.

In the midst of this wonderful marriage that was headed to forever, Lisa was totally unprepared for John's battle with cancer. His death, after twenty-two years of marriage, left Lisa without the chance to grow old with John. Her dream had ended. Sometimes she can't express how much she misses him. Yet God has revealed to Lisa His new purpose for her life.

During these last five years, she has listened to neglected people, poured hope into the hearts of the hopeless, taught the Word of God, and provided leadership in her church.

We may have hopes and dreams of what our lives will look like. Ultimately, God's plan unfolds. Then we have two choices. We can feel resentful if His plan isn't what we wanted. Or we can choose to be grateful and thankful to God for His plan, knowing it flows out of His love for us.

When we're grateful, we open the way to believe by faith that the circumstances we face are from the Lord, and He will bring good out of them.

In Colossians 4:2, the apostle Paul reminds believers to "devote yourselves to prayer with an alert mind and a thankful heart."

I often repeat 1 Thessalonians 5:18: "Be thankful in all circumstances, for this is God's will for you who belong to Christ Jesus."

Lisa told me her commitment to gratitude and thankfulness creates a positive and hopeful perspective each day and prevents negative thinking.

A Heart of Gratitude

We can all thank God for His assurance that He will walk with us for the rest of our lives.

What are you grateful for today?

My Personal Prayer:

_____

_____

_____

_____

_____

_____

_____

_____

_____

_____

Bible Memory Verse:

Be thankful in all circumstances, for this is God's will for you who belong to Christ Jesus. (1 Thessalonians 5:18)

Chapter Challenge:

- Are you still in the grieving season from the loss of a loved one? Do you have a family member or close friend who prays for you, spends time with you, and is available to listen? If not, reach out to someone you know who will understand, or ask God to bring a caring person into your life. Remember, you are never alone. God is there with you.

- What blessing do you want to thank God for today? Spend some time in prayer and thank Him for that blessing, which is a gift from Him. Ask the Lord to fill your heart with gratitude day by day.

_____

_____

_____

_____

_____

_____

- Think of people you can encourage this week. Invite someone for coffee or a meal in your home or favorite restaurant. Call someone or go for a walk with them. Perhaps mail a card or send a text. Ask God to bring a person across your path who needs your encouraging smile and words.

Chapter 12

Following His Lead
Gail Porter

Can you identify with one of the stories you've read?
Perhaps. Maybe more than one. Or did one section, one phrase, or one word grip your heart?

No matter which story relates best to our own situations, one element is universal: life is a series of ups and downs. Never a simple, straight line. We'd like life to consist of nothing but high points. However, it never will be.

The ten people who courageously shared their personal stories in this book know this truth. Each story embraces heartache and disappointment, and most describe darkness and devastation. Yet they're amazing stories of survival. From the darkness, hope arises when someone is rescued from bondage, redeemed from all they'd lost, and transformed into a new person.

Into those lives of hopelessness came a shining light of hope—the light of Jesus Christ. Each person's story of redemption is astounding.

God never left any of these people alone. He stayed by their sides, enduring heartache with them. He knew the exact moment freedom would triumph over evil, and they would embrace a personal relationship with His Son, Jesus. God set each one free to tell others not to give up but to hang on to hope.

God led them to the path of freedom, where they could travel for the rest of their lives. He began revealing who He designed them to be and how they could live, thrive, and focus on God's unique purposes for them.

New Understanding

My journey of becoming the person God intended me to be began when I opened my heart to Him at the student meeting on my college campus. I was already familiar with God and Jesus Christ, because I went to church with my family. However, I didn't know much about the Holy Spirit.

Through my study group on campus and personal Bible studies, I learned that God put His Holy Spirit inside me when I began my personal relationship with God. The Holy Spirit would be with me for the rest of my life, showing me how to follow God's plans for me.

I discovered that the Holy Spirit cautions me when I'm about to make a wrong decision and comforts me when sadness comes. As I give Him control of my life day by day, He fills me with His power to live the way God intended. Through His guidance, I become more and more the person God created me to be.

I began to understand that God is three Persons in One:

3. God the Father: my Creator, who breathed life into me and set His eternal plan into motion. He is with me always, knows everything about me before it takes place, and connects me with people He wants me to meet.

4. God the Son: my Savior, Jesus Christ, who died on the cross to save me from my sins by paying the penalty I deserved. When I accepted His sacrifice for me, He gave me the privilege of living eternally with Him in heaven.

5. God the Holy Spirit: my Counselor, who lives inside me and

helps me follow God's eternal plan. The Holy Spirit will be my Companion for the rest of my life.

The following verse (Jesus's conversation with His disciples before He returned to heaven) gave me a picture of the loving interrelationship of the Father, the Son, and the Holy Spirit (the Helper).

> [Jesus said,] I will ask the Father, and He will give you another Helper, so that He may be with you forever; the Helper is the Spirit of truth, whom the world cannot receive, because it does not see Him or know Him; but you know Him because He remains with you and will be in you. (John 14:16–17 NASB)

A Matter of Commitment

While still in college, I sensed the Holy Spirit speaking to my heart about my commitment to God. As I walked across our beautiful campus quad, the Holy Spirit put into my mind that I had given God control of most of my life, but not all. As I pondered this thought, the Lord showed me that I was holding on to control of two specific areas of my life: my relationship with my current boyfriend and my future career.

This revelation stunned me. Needing a private place to process, I pivoted on the walkway and headed toward the majestic Student Memorial Union. Near the back of the expansive room full of students studying for midterms, I spotted an empty cushioned chair near a window that overlooked a corner of the sprawling campus.

Having reached my destination, I placed my spiral notebook and textbooks on the side table. I reached into my bag and grabbed my personal notepad and small Bible. Curled up on the soft burgundy chair, I bowed my head.

I silently prayed and confessed my sin to God and willingly relinquished control of my relationship with my boyfriend and my career. Then I whispered, "I trust You with my whole life." Immediately, I sensed relief from the weight of trying to orchestrate my own life.

When I began committing myself to the Holy Spirit and allowing

Him to fill me with His power each day, I felt steady, assured, and unafraid of what the day might bring. My life centered on God and others, because I accepted His plans and let go of my nearsighted, predictable, shallow, and self-made plans.

Now I read God's Word every morning. His Word reveals truth, which is my protection against the lies of the enemy. I praise the Lord for who He is and what He has done in my life the previous day or week before presenting my needs or expressing my struggles.

I ask the Holy Spirit to take control of my day so I won't hinder His plans. When I forget, the Holy Spirit reminds me so I can confess and start following God again. I often ask Him to keep me alert to His prompts so I won't miss anything He wants me to experience.

What if I had ignored the Holy Spirit's instructions to join the Cru ministry and instead had followed my own plan to become a business-woman? Years later, I stood at the crossroads of decision, wondering if I should retire and begin my personal ministry or stay with Cru. What if I had ignored the Holy Spirit's leading to a new life of freedom because I didn't want to risk the possibility of failure?

I'll always be grateful that the Holy Spirit gave me courage to step out in faith and fully embrace His perfect plan for my life. I pray I will keep listening to the Holy Spirit and follow Him wherever He leads.

> LORD, You are my God; I will exalt You, I will give thanks to Your name; for You have worked wonders, plans formed long ago, with perfect faithfulness. (Isaiah 25:1 NASB)

Living in Freedom

God has unimaginable plans for you. When you come out of your hiding place, tear down your defenses, and leave your fear of rejection behind, He will lead you to the path of freedom. There you will experience hope for your future, along with joy and peace you never thought possible.

I pray that God, the source of hope, will fill you completely with joy and peace because you trust in him. Then you will overflow with confident hope through the power of the Holy Spirit. (Romans 15:13)

No matter what you have been through, God will bring beauty out of your ashes so others can see His work in your life and truly believe they can receive redemption and healing for themselves.

I'll meet you on the path of freedom.

Gail

A NOTE FROM THE AUTHOR

When I read books like this, I wonder how they evolved. This book began with a nudge from God. He gave me the idea of showing readers how life could look on God's path of freedom.

My heart embraced this concept because it represented my passion, but I wondered where to find the stories. In what seemed like only moments, God dropped names into my mind. Then He brought other people across my path, and they told me their stories of rejection. Their ten stories became part of this book.

What intrigued me most was that each of these ten people are my personal friends. I didn't seek them out; God gave each one to me. I've known some of them a long time. Others are newer friends. However, they all experienced the results of rejection and now live a life of freedom.

Something unexpected happened after they told their stories. A handful felt relieved to learn they could finally reveal their lifelong secrets. Others realized they had experienced the fulfillment of a dream that one day they could tell their personal life stories.

Several uncovered deeply buried emotions and trauma. Once exposed, these new discoveries expanded their sense of freedom.

My greatest delight has been to see redemption emerge from their tragic lives of rejection. God now uses their past pain and their new lives of freedom to show others they, too, can walk away from rejection and live free.

Spending time with these dear storytellers changed my life. Perhaps reading their stories will change yours.

www.gailporterauthor.com

OTHER BOOKS BY GAIL

*Does fear of rejection hold you back
from letting people know you?
Are you tired of hiding?*

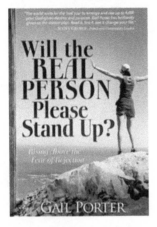

*It is possible to find God's path of freedom
where you can become the Real You.*

PAPERBACK AND E-BOOK
Redemption Press:
gailporterauthor.com/RP-rejection-book
Amazon:
gailporterauthor.com/Amazon-rejection-book

PAPERBACK AND
DOWNLOADABLE FACILITATOR GUIDE
Redemption Press:
gailporterauthor.com/RP-womens-weekend-retreat
Amazon:
gailporterauthor.com/Amazon-womens-weekend-retreat

*Life may be waiting for you
just around the bend.
Take the next step.*

PAPERBACK AND E-BOOK
Amazon:
gailporterauthor.com/Amazon-Life-through-Loss

ACKNOWLEDGMENTS

I want to thank the wonderful team at Redemption Press. Special thanks to Christina Miller, my writing coach who walked alongside me each step of my journey. This book, which continually evolved in unexpected ways, became a reality because of your expert coaching. I'll be forever grateful for your wisdom, patience, encouragement, and amazing ability to help me bring truth out of each story so readers could find freedom.

Without the ten people who courageously revealed their deep and personal stories of rejection and redemption, this book would not exist. Thank you for saying yes to the call of God and allowing Him to change lives through you.

Thank you to many friends who believed in this project, provided encouragement at the right moments, became advisers and sounding boards when needed, and prayed for perseverance to move forward and complete this assignment God entrusted to me.

To my Father God, my loving Lord, and my Holy Spirit Companion, thank You for surrounding me daily, filling me with Your words, and showing me Your desire for each chapter. Thank You for the privilege of becoming part of Your plan to reach people in bondage and set them free.

About Gail

GAIL PORTER relishes her many opportunities to visit and minister in various countries during her fifty years of service with Cru in the US and Asia. Now involved in her own ministry in Orlando, she loves writing, speaking about her journey to freedom, and fulfilling her passion of helping people realize they can be free of their fear of rejection and live authentic lives.

Gail is the award-winning author of *Will the Real Person Please Stand Up: Rising Above the Fear of Rejection; Free to be the Real You: A Women's Weekend Retreat;* and *Life Through Loss: Facing Your Pain, Finding Your Purpose.* Order her newest book, *Living on the Path of Freedom: Leaving Fear of Rejection Behind,* through Redemption Press (redemption-press.com/product/living-on-the-path-of-freedom)

To learn more about Gail and her books, visit her website: gailporterauthor.com

Blog: gailporterauthor.com/blog
Email: contact@gailporterauthor.com
Facebook: Facebook.com/gail.porter.731
YouTube Channel: gailporterauthor.com/YouTube
Have you taken the Fear of Rejection Quiz?
gailporterauthor.com/quiz

Order Information

To order additional copies of this book,
please visit www.redemption-press.com.
Also available at Christian bookstores
and BarnesandNoble.com
or by calling toll-free 1-844-2REDEEM.

Printed in the USA
CPSIA information can be obtained
at www.ICGtesting.com
JSHW021925290723
45532JS00001B/2